I0792081

The Dead Truth

STORIES FROM BEHIND THE WALL

C. E. Adminis

ARCHWAY
PUBLISHING

Archway Publishing books may be ordered through booksellers or by contacting:

Archway Publishing
1663 Liberty Drive
Bloomington, IN 47403
www.archwaypublishing.com
844-669-3957

ISBN: 978-1-6657-3433-2 (sc)
ISBN: 978-1-6657-3434-9 (e)

Library of Congress Control Number: 2022922513

Print information available on the last page.

Archway Publishing rev. date: 01/10/2023

Contents

Introduction

The average person has no idea what happens in juvenile hall, county jails, and state prisons. This included me until I started working in the penal system. I was somewhat naïve as to the things that go on behind these walls, but I was more surprised at what I heard, witnessed, and experienced. Before working in these different facilities, I was of the impression that, with my background and skills as a coach, teacher, and mentor, I would be able to have an immediate impact on the lives of those who were incarcerated and help them to grow and change and become productive citizens in our society.

I believed that, with my teaching skills, I would be able to help the inmates with their studies. With my coaching skills, I thought I could motivate them to move forward with their lives. And with my mentoring skills, I was sure I could advise and assist these people in turning their lives in a different direction. I truly believed that I could reach almost anyone and would be able to make it easy for them to change their ways.

It was not until I started working on the *inside* (juvenile hall) that I came to realize that I knew absolutely nothing about the criminal mind. The dead truth was that I was clueless about the way the criminal mind works.

For example, most if not all inmates—juveniles and adults—believed they did not deserve to be incarcerated. And they believed that the crimes they had committed were not that bad. There were those who believed that what they had done should not be a crime at all and that the laws were wrong and should be changed. Why do criminals think this way? Who knows for sure?

I'm sure that a contributing factor is that the average age of a convict is thirty-six years old. Most have a fourth- or fifth-grade reading level and a third- or fourth-grade math level. With little or no education, many of these people have minimal job prospects. In addition, their reasoning skills are often of low quality (taking us back to the criminal mind).

The convict's living environment also comes into consideration. Some people from poor communities are more prone to commit crimes. Do the lifestyles of the ghettos, barrios, and trailer parks cause the criminal mind to think this way? Or is this behavior learned from older criminals who are committing crimes that the young, up-and-coming ones want to emulate? Or is criminality taught and handed down from generation to generation?

Then there are the wannabees. These (mostly) juveniles come from middle-class families and want the attention "thugs" and "bad boys" get from girls and others. They do things just to get attention, and they don't care about the consequences because they believe that, whatever happens, their parents will get them out of trouble. This is sad but true.

The truth is that the criminal mindset results from a combination of all the above. However, with many juveniles, I believe it is a fifty-fifty split. Some juveniles have an above-average educational level but are influenced by the gold, cars, and cash flashed by drug dealers. Others are being raised by grandparents or foster parents and think that the only way to have *stuff* is to get involved in crime. Also, there is family dynamics: perhaps mother, father, uncles, cousins, and siblings have been incarcerated so it is a badge of honor to follow in their footsteps.

A myriad of circumstances contribute to the criminal mind, and many are still unknown.

The stories you are about to read are about situations I personally observed, experiences I was personally involved with, or situations I learned about through discussions with correctional officers, parole agents, and teachers under my supervision. These stories are true. Some are funny, some are disgusting, some are cruel, and some are deadly. But they are accurate; I have told them as I remember them.

Many criminals believe that the crimes they commit will work because they think they have planned them well and they will not get caught. They are not aware that their reasoning skills are flawed. Many believe that what they are about to do has never been done before. Some suffer from delusions of grandeur.

Most human beings typically do not think about spending any time in jail or prison. However, there are those who prefer being behind the wall that curtails their freedom.

Prior to my employment experience in corrections, I had no idea that people like the ones I encountered existed. Working behind the wall brought me face to face with the criminal mind and so much more.

Read on and be enlightened.

How Did I Get Caught?

How Did I Get So Far Gone?

—Curtis Mayfield

Keistered

Prison is a totally different animal than jail or juvenile hall. The routine is different, and the people are really different.

I worked in a prison as the administrator of a drug education program. There were fourteen teachers who provided classes in life skills, drug education, parenting, and many other skills to the parolees in this program. In the evenings, there was an opportunity for independent study, and the parolees had one-on-one independent study with a teacher. In lieu of going back to prison to serve their full terms, which could mean at least one year, they were given the option of attending this ninety-day drug education program. It was a three-phase program. Upon graduation, they would have the option of attending an after-care program that provided room and board for ninety days while they looked for work.

The parolees who were allowed to come to this program were non-violent, low-level offenders who had drug issues. Although this program was for parolees, it took place inside a prison, and I was told that prison rules applied. Initially, I was not aware what they meant by "prison rules," but I was quick to learn it meant inmates were segregated by race. There was no mixing. Whites were with Whites. Blacks were with Blacks. Hispanics were with Hispanics, Asians were with Asians, and so on. This was a little difficult for me to understand at first because, when these same people were on the streets together, they drank from the same bottle and slept next door to one another. But when they came to prison, all their activities were separated based on race.

One of the ways contraband is smuggled into a prison is through "keistering"—shoving the item to be smuggled up the butt. This usually happens upon initial arrival, but it can happen when an inmate has gone out on a medical appointment or for some other reason.

This story is about an inmate who had been in the program for forty-five days and was doing well. He was a good student, did not cause any problems, and was helpful to his teachers. He got word from his parole agent that his mother had passed. He put in a request to me to be granted a five-hour unsupervised release from the program to attend his mother's funeral. This was not an unusual request, as this was a very low-level prison that housed nonviolent offenders. I discussed this with the lieutenant and the on-site parole agents. Because of his good record in the program, we all agreed to allow him to attend his mother's funeral. He emphasized that he had only another forty-five days left in the program and had worked hard. He stated he was very close to his mother and needed to attend her funeral as support for his two younger siblings.

His temporary release was granted, and he was able to attend the funeral. Upon his return, he was aware that he would be strip searched and urine tested to ensure that he had brought no contraband into the prison, and he had not used drugs while he was out. This was where the criminogenic thinking of this parolee had taken over. He assumed that, because this was (in his mind) not a *real* prison, the correctional officers would not notice if he keistered a few balloons of marijuana.

He thought he would get away with it. It seemed that he just knew he would not get caught.

After the parolee was searched, he put his prison clothes on and walked to his bed area. However, the sharp eye of one of the correctional officers noticed that the parolee seemed to walking with a different gait. He logged his observation and shared his suspicions with the other staff members and the staff members who were coming on the next shift. Now the next-shift staff members were watching this inmate. When the morning shift came on duty, they were informed of what had been observed by the other officers and what they thought this inmate had done. They all felt this inmate had keistered something. They waited for the inmate to go to the bathroom that morning, and when he reached his hand into the toilet to retrieve the balloons—surprise!—he was busted. This inmate had the typical criminogenic response when caught: "How'd you know? I didn't think you guys would notice me! How'd you catch me?"

Unfortunately, from that point on, no one else was allowed to leave the facility regardless of the reasons or circumstances. And this guy was charged with bringing drugs into the prison and was given an additional eighteen-month sentence.

Sex with the Psychologist

The Boys Ranch facility is open and surrounded by farmland. There was a time when they raised cows, chickens, and other farm animals. They grew vegetables that were served in the kitchen. When the kids started to mutilate the animals and destroy the plants they grew, all these programs were removed.

During the week, there was a full staff—school principal; six teachers; nurse; administrator; psychologist; a couple of supervisors; two support staff; and, on average, ten counselors. The role of the psychologist in this juvenile environment was to deliver psychological healthcare to the youth who were incarcerated. He was supposed to assess, diagnose, and treat the psychological problems, behavioral problems, and behavioral dysfunctions that resulted from or were related to physical and mental health issues. He was not supposed to be a sexual predator.

Unfortunately, this guy was something out of some weird novel. We will call him Doctor Step. He wasn't from around that part of the country and had lived in the area for only about fifteen years. He had worked at the facility for about three years. I do not know where he came from or what he had done before coming to this facility. He seemed to be a nice guy, but now we know that was a façade. Using his position as facility psychologist, he used these kids' issues to manipulate them for his own sexual pleasure. No one really knows how long he had been abusing these kids, but he became so secure in what he was doing that he got careless.

First, he made a slight change to his work schedule. His normal schedule, like the schedule for teachers, nurses, support staff, and the administrator, was Monday through Friday, eight in the morning to four in the afternoon. Counselors were on site twenty-four seven. One Saturday morning, the counselors noticed that Doctor Step was on site. When he was questioned, he stated that he had to catch up on some paperwork. He knew that, on Saturdays and Sundays, the only staff members on site were seven to ten counselors, and that number was dependent on how many juvenile inmates were in residence. The fact that there were no teachers, no support staff, no nurses, and no administrator on site made his Saturday visits easier. After the first Saturday, none of the staff members paid much attention to him, so he made it a habit to come in on Saturdays. His story was that it was easier to see the kids on Saturday because there was no school, and that meant fewer interruptions. He could really work with the kids. One other observation about his Saturday visits was that the blinds in his office were always closed, which was suspicious. Yes, he was really working these young boys.

When the administrator found out that Doctor Step was working on Saturdays without requesting a change in his schedule, he became suspicious. Additionally, the doctor's timecard showed him working Monday through Friday with no mention of Saturday work—a stupid mistake. This also increased the administrator's suspicions. He had the files of Doctor Step reviewed to determine which inmates he was seeing on Saturdays. To the administrator's surprise, there were no records of this guy seeing any kids on Saturdays. Yet he was always there on Saturdays with kids in his office, and with the blinds closed—another stupid mistake. At this point, the administrator decided to set up an observation operation. One Saturday, Doctor Step came to work and called a juvenile into his office. After a short period of time, the supervisor who had been instructed to observe Doctor Step, entered the office. He caught the doctor with his pants down having sex with this minor. Doctor Step was handcuffed and arrested. The administrator was called, and an incident report was made. The juvenile admitted he was a regular with Doctor Step, and there were others. The files of all the doctor's sex victims included a mention of homosexual tendencies, and he had used this information for his own pleasure.

After his arrest, he asked that age old question: "How did you find out?" It appears that Doctor Step did not think that he would get caught. The truth is, no matter how much education you have, if you commit a crime, you will eventually get caught.

Teacher Having Sex with Students

Working the day shift on a weekday was different from working on the weekends. Our weekday routine went like this: We got the kids up in the morning and got them ready for breakfast. We took them to breakfast, and then we took them back to the dorm to allow them to brush their teeth and get ready for school. We moved them out to school, and then we waited for the school break. When the boys took a break, they would come back to the dorm, use the bathroom, and then we would return them back to class after about fifteen minutes. At lunch time, we moved them from the school to the dorm, allowed them to wash up, and then moved them to the lunch facility. After lunch, we moved them back to the dorm to allow them to brush their teeth and wash up. After a one-hour lunch break, we then moved them from the dorm back to school. After school, we moved the kids back to the dorm. There would be a couple of hours before the youths were taken to have dinner, so there would be a quiet hour, and we would again sit and wait.

All the adults working on the inside were not always who they claimed to be. The teacher in this story was not a bad-looking lady—middle aged, a little plump, and somewhat homely. She was single, lived with her mother, and loved cats. She had pictures of her cats all around her classroom. Before working at this juvenile facility, she had worked at a local high school as a substitute teacher. She now had a permanent job working as a teacher at this juvenile facility, and she had worked there for a couple of years.

Her students seemed to like her and always wanted to do things for her. She had a few favorites, but no one suspected her of doing anything illicit or unsavory with her students. It is not known how many students she was having sex with or how long it had been going on, and no one suspected that it was happening. Looking at her, no one would fathom that this was something within her, but it was. As I said earlier, she had her favorites, and we found out later that there were four of them. Well, these favorites were the kids she was routinely having sex with. Each one had his day with her.

You are probably wondering how she got caught. Think about this for just a few minutes—you are a fifteen- or sixteen-year-old kid, you are locked in a juvenile facility with no girls, and you are having sex with an older woman on a regular basis. Young boys always brag about their conquests, especially if it is with an older woman. When a few of the other boys heard about this, they wanted some of the action too. They approached the teacher and told her that they wanted to be included as one of her favorites. She acted as if she had no idea what they were talking about and blew them off. This did not sit well with these juvenile delinquents, and they decided that, if they could not be involved, then no one else would either. A couple of the boys who had been turned down informed the supervisors what was happening, when it was happening, how it was happening, and who was involved. These staff members informed the administrator who instructed the counselors and supervisors to surveil this teacher and try to catch her in the act.

Several staff members waited until the time they had been led to believe when the sex would take place. They walked in on her having sex with a juvenile on her desk. She was busted with her dress up and panties down. She was a female sexual predator. To my surprise, I learned that not all sexual predators are male.

Here again that same old question: "How did you find out?" The answer to this query is easy. As an adult, you cannot do stupid stuff with young boys and expect to get away with it.

Teacher Having a Relationship with a Parolee at Large

This was a normal day at my classrooms at the prison. All the teachers were on time, and there were no issues in any of the eight classrooms that I was responsible for. It was almost lunchtime, and I was waiting for my parole agents to complete intake forms for new parolees who were on their way to the facility. As I was walking to my car to go to lunch, I got a call on my cell phone from a friend of mine who was the parole administrator for another area. He said to me, "What the hell is wrong with your teachers?" I had no idea what he was talking about because all my teachers were in class doing their work with their students. He continued with the conversation telling me about a teacher and a parolee at large (PAL), or fugitive.

You would think that being a teacher—earning a college degree and going through the teacher credentialing process—would make a person smarter than the average criminal. Well, you can say teachers are people too and can be influenced to lean toward the dark side. This is so true in this story of a teacher and a PAL. This teacher fell deep into the depths of the dark side. Here is the story.

This teacher taught drug education and life skills to parolees in a parole office in a different part of the state. He was a tall, nice-looking man in his mid-forties. There was something strange about him because he would never associate with other teachers when we had training sessions, especially with the female teachers. He was arrogant and led people believe that he knew everything. At our last training session, he would not follow the procedures we were being trained on and told everyone that he was used to doing things differently in his classroom. This was cause for concern for his immediate supervisor and parole staff. As teachers in parole offices, we had to follow certain protocols, and he was reluctant to do so. Unknown to his colleagues, supervisors, and parole agents, this teacher was a drug user on the downlow. In addition, he was having a homosexual relationship with a parolee in his class.

You are probably curious as to how this all came to light. It all started when a parolee stopped attending class and stopped reporting to his parole officer. It had been well over thirty days since anyone had seen him or he'd had any contact with his parole officer. Because of his long absence, he was considered to be a fugitive or parolee at large. Because he was a PAL and a violent offender, many agencies were looking for him: police personnel, sheriff's personnel, and the fugitive apprehension team (FAT).

It took close to six months to finally locate this parolee, and he had been hiding in plain sight. The parolee and another male had been observed entering a home. Authorities surrounded the home and knocked on the front door. The male who answered the door was the teacher from the parole office. He was asked to let the agent see the parolee whom they had observed entering the residence with him. The teacher lied and said no one by that name was in the home. When the agent insisted and explained that he and his team had observed the parolee enter the house with him, the teacher attempted to block the door. The agents forced their way into the house, and the teacher yelled to the parolee, "Run!"

Because the house was surrounded, the parolee was apprehended when he attempted to run out the backdoor. The teacher was also arrested for harboring a fugitive. Upon searching the residence, they found weapons, drugs, drug paraphernalia, stolen property, pornography, and a number of other illegal items. The teacher was charged along with the parolee for all the contraband found in the house. It was also noted that there was only one bed in the house, so it was assumed that they were having a homosexual affair.

As the teacher was being led away that question was asked again: "How did you know the parolee was here?" As I have stated before, education does not make a person a smart criminal.

Sex with the Twelve-Year-Old Stepdaughter

When a person is incarcerated, a phone call, in many cases, is the only direct connection to those at home, although some may receive letters and those who are incarcerated close to home may get visits from family members. It is a known fact that all calls going out of prison are monitored and recorded. You would think that anyone with common sense would remember this and not say anything that would get him into trouble. However, on this particular day, this inmate must have had a total brain freeze.

The inmate was a forty-five-year-old Black male. He was a small-time drug dealer and drug user, he was married, and he had a twelve-year-old stepdaughter. By all indications, they were a happy family. On some Sundays, his wife and her daughter would visit him at the facility.

In the drug education program, there was a graduation ceremony every sixty to ninety days or so. Students who had successfully completed the program were honored in a ceremony. They wore caps and gowns and received certificates of completion from the program. Many of these parolees had never completed anything in their lives, so this was an accomplishment for them. When the ceremony was over, cake and punch were provided for all the graduates, and then the other students were given cake and punch as well. After the festivities, the inmates were sent back to their dorms and allowed to do what they normally did in the evenings. Some would write letters, and others would use the phone.

This parolee was one of the better students in the program. He was a teacher's aide who helped other students complete their assignments, and in the evenings, he would assist students with their homework. During the interactions I had with him, there was no indication that he was a pedophile or predator.

One afternoon, I was called to the dorm where the parole agents had their office and was instructed to listen to a recorded phone conversation this parolee had with his family. The phone call started normally as the parolee talked to his wife and asked how things were at home. He told her that he had just graduated from the program and would be home in a few days. After the conversation with his wife, he asked to speak with his stepdaughter. This is when the phone call took a downward spin. Actually, it became downright nasty. He started the conversation by asking the child if she missed her daddy and how much she missed him. The child responded that she missed him a lot. He continued his conversation by asking her how she wanted her daddy to give it to her when he got home. Oops! What is that about? Next, he asked what position she missed the most—was it her on top of him, him on top of her, or did she like him doing it to her from the back better. The conversation this guy was having with his twelve-year-old stepdaughter would embarrass some long-time pedophiles. Did he not realize that his conversation was being recorded? Did he not realize that the conversation with his stepdaughter was inappropriate?

After I was allowed to hear this conversation, prison and parole investigators were given the tapes. When the investigators reviewed the tape, they were shocked that an inmate would have such an open conversation on a prison phone and would be talking to a young child in such a way.

The investigators had to move quickly because he was being released from the program in a few days, and they did not want him to get home and continue molesting his stepdaughter. They went to the home of this suspected pedophile and had a conversation with his wife and her daughter. The mother was unaware that her husband had been sexually molesting her daughter. She was extremely angry and said that she wanted him to rot in prison. She said she was filing for divorce immediately and never wanted to see him again.

When they arrested him by his bed he asked, "What did I do? I've been locked up for the past three months and could not have done anything!"

When he was told what he was being charged with he asked, "How did you find out?" The officers reminded him that all phone calls at the prison were monitored and recorded. They explained to him that they had also spoken with his wife and his stepdaughter, and that the child had told them what he had been doing to her for the past year every time her mother went to work. She also stated that she was afraid to say no to him for fear that he would hurt her.

Whether it was arrogance or stupidity, the molester's "brain freeze" got him just what he deserved—he was locked up. It also rescued a twelve-year-old child from further trauma.

Defecation in the Van

History tells us that most criminals are not smart, and they believe that they can always get away with breaking the law even after they have been caught. After they are caught and are doing their time in prison, the inmates make comments like, "I'll do it differently the next time so I won't get caught" or "I have a better plan for next time, one that no one has done before." The average person believes just the opposite; they fear getting caught and going to jail, and they know that most plans have been tried. The proof is that previous offenders are incarcerated.

The average person thinks before he acts. He uses his critical thinking skills to determine if it is worth the risk getting caught just to do something stupid. However, the average criminal usually acts before he or she thinks without considering the consequences of his or her actions.

Additionally, many criminals believe that the law does not pertain to them, and when they are caught, they feel that they have been wronged and the laws should be changed. With this mentality, many criminals have revenge on their minds—revenge against the police, parole agents, all law enforcement agencies, and the government in its entirety. They want to get back at all those they feel put them where they are. They do not accept accountability for the fact they put themselves there by breaking the law.

The parolee in this story was one of those people. He hated the system, and he believed that everyone involved had wronged him at every turn regardless of his actions and the crimes he had committed. His criminal file was larger than an old phone book; it went back to when he was first arrested at age thirteen for breaking into a home and beating the elderly occupants.

He was a forty-year-old White male who came from a very poor family background. He never finished high school, but he was fairly intelligent. He was a bully and thought he knew more than the people around him, which was part of his problem.

Because of a parole violation, he was sent to my ninety-day, in-prison drug education program. In the program, he did what he was told to do and did not cause any problems. He complained to other inmates about things he did not like, but he was smart enough to understand that all he had to do was complete the program in ninety days, and he would go home.

This parolee did his time, graduated from the program, gave a speech saying he appreciated the program, and said he looked forward to starting a new chapter in his life because he had learned so much from the program.

When parolees are released from the program and they do not have a ride home, they are transported to an after-care facility (if they choose to go to one) or to their parole office. This parolee was being transported to his parole office along with five other parolees. He had a place to live and a job waiting for him, so he did not need to go to an aftercare program. He was the last parolee to be dropped off at the parole office. After he was dropped off and the agents were returning the van back to the prison yard, they smelled something in the van that did not smell right. When they arrived back at the prison yard, they looked in the rear of the van to determine the source of the smell. In the back of the van where the last parolee had been sitting, they discovered that source. Yes, the last parolee had defecated in the rear of the van.

The parole agents knew who had committed this despicable act, but unfortunately, because no one saw him do it, they didn't have enough evidence to arrest him.

The parole agents called the supervisor at the parole office where they had dropped off the inmate and informed him of the situation. The agents wanted the supervisor to bring up the incident to see what kind of response he would get from the parolee.

Remember, criminals are really not very smart, and they like to brag about doing something illegal when they think they have gotten away with it. As this guy was sitting in the parole office talking to other parolees he knew, he began to brag about the fact that he had just defecated in the back of the transport van, and the authorities could not prove he had done it. He had everyone around him laughing. He just knew that he had gotten away with this act of disrespect. Even though he was telling everyone sitting in the parole office what he had done, he knew that no one there would snitch on him. The convict oath is "snitches get stitches." However, he had no idea that a plainclothes police officer was waiting to talk with a supervisor. When the police officer went inside, he informed the supervisor what he had heard.

When it was time for the parolee to report to the supervisor, he was asked about the incident in the van. The parolee denied any involvement and attempted to blame others who were riding in the van with him. Obviously, he thought that all the people in the waiting room were just parolees, and he knew that they would not say anything. When the supervisor asked the police officer to come into the office, the parolee almost passed out. He said, "Why weren't you in your cop's uniform? If I knew you were a cop, I would have kept my mouth shut."

He had just completed ninety days in an in-prison program, and now he was looking at a minimum of a year in prison. You never know who is listening. Criminals are *not smart*!

Caught in the Shower

This day was not an unusual day in the prison except for the fact that one of the inmates we received was a homosexual who flaunted the fact that he was gay. He walked around the dorm area and smiled and blew kisses to some of the inmates he knew from other prisons. He was not the first gay man we had in the program, but he was the first to openly display the fact that he was gay. I was not sure what to think or how to react, so I did not react in any way.

Homosexual affairs are against prison rules, but they happen all the time. When talking to inmates about sexual acts, many will make the statement, "I'm only gay in prison." I did not quite understand what that meant because, in my mind, a homosexual is a homosexual regardless of where he is. Rarely will anyone admit to having a homosexual affair, but it happens all the time, and staff members are usually the last to know or they ignore the rumors, but they will respond if they witness the act.

This is a story about one instance when an inmate wanted sex from a gay inmate. The parolee was a Black male about thirty-eight years old. He was married, and he and his wife had three kids. He was a small-time drug dealer and user. He had been in the program for only a little less than thirty days. I was not sure what his issues were, but whatever they were, they came out. He told us that he heard through the prison grapevine that a particular gay inmate was good at giving oral sex, and he wanted a turn. The gay parolee was a thirty-two-year-old, slender biracial man who had been arrested multiple times for prostitution and drug sales. He was new to the program; he had only been there for three weeks. He had already gained the reputation of being a "free loving gay man."

When the parolee approached the gay inmate, he asked to have sex with him but was turned down. The gay parolee also told him he already had a special man. This upset the other parolee and made him determined to find out who this special man was. When he found out who the special man was, he beat him up to get him out of the picture believing he would take his place. No one was willing to tell who had beat this guy up for fear of repercussions; however, when the gay parolee found out who was responsible for beating up his boyfriend, he told staff and continued to refuse the other man's advances.

Unfortunately, the inmate who wanted sex was kicked out of the program and sent to another prison to do a one-year term. When I asked him why he had beat the guy up, he stated, "He was having sex with him and others, but would not have sex with me. If I could not have him, no one else was going to have him either." I asked him if he knew what the consequences were going to be. He said yes, and he really did not care because he knew where he would be going. I asked him why he could not wait about sixty days to be released so he could go back to his wife. He said, "My wife does not like to do oral sex." This is just one story of homosexuality in prison.

This next story—the shower story—is really nasty. In this particular prison facility, we added shower curtains so that the inmates could have a little privacy. One morning at about 7:40, twenty minutes before classes were to start, I heard the shower running. Showers were to be completed by 7:30. I yelled up for this individual to get out and get ready for class. There was no response. I headed up the stairs to get the inmate moving, and another inmate, who had heard me yell, followed me toward the shower. As I approached the shower, the inmate who had followed me opened the curtain.

To our surprise, there were two inmates in the shower. One was standing. He was a forty-four-year-old married man who had six kids. He stood six foot two and weighed 250 pounds. The other man was on his knees. He was a thirty-three-year-old chubby gay man. He was taking the big guy's penis out of his mouth and was spitting out semen.

The inmate who opened the shower curtain was a friend of the man who was standing. He yelled, "You nasty motherfucker! Other people use this shower, and you let this dick sucking motherfucker spit that shit on the shower floor where we have to stand? I'm calling your fucking wife and telling her that her fucking husband is a faggot and is having this other faggot suck his dick in the prison shower! You should be ashamed of yourself!" The inmate who was standing said, "If you had not opened the damn curtain, no one would have known, and I would not have been caught." He showed no accountability and no remorse regarding his wife and kids. He just expressed misguided frustration about being caught. There is no accounting for the idiocy of the criminal mind.

2

CHAPTER

Institutionalized

What's Going On.

—"What's Going On," Marvin Gaye, Renaldo
Benson, and Al Cleveland

Normal people would reject the idea of having to spend time in jail or prison; however, there are those who, at times, would rather be in jail or prison than be free. Being a normal person, I had no idea that there were people—adults and juveniles of both genders—who felt that going to jail or prison was no big thing. As you read the following stories, you will get a glimpse of some of these people and why they felt the need to be incarcerated.

I Like It Here

It was my first day on the job as a juvenile probation counselor. I was going through my orientation week, and I was assigned a juvenile to show me around the facility and introduce me to the staff members.

My chaperone was a chubby little White kid around sixteen years old; he could have been an altar boy.

I assumed that, because this kid had been chosen to be my escort, he must be doing things right. This setting was new to me, so I felt the need to read the files of the juveniles I encountered to understand who they were, where they came from, and what they had done to get locked up. The file on my chaperone was rather thick for a sixteen-year-old.

Reading it, I saw that there were no violent crimes or major incidents. His crimes were mostly small things—marijuana possession, petty theft, public intoxication—but no serious crimes. However, the crimes he did commit were enough to get him time in a juvenile facility. This was the fifth time in less than two years that he had been sent to the Boys Ranch. He was never sentenced to any long stretch, and he was always given a program and not a mandatory sentence.

Being sentenced to a program meant that, for every day a juvenile had that was free of incidents, he earned a day of freedom. For example, if a juvenile was sentenced to a ninety-day program and he was incident free for forty-five days, he could go home after forty-five days and not have to spend the remaining forty-five days in juvenile detention. This was true for all programs regardless of the length. After reading his file, I noticed that he always did his full term. He never earned any days for good behavior, but he was involved in an incident that would cause him to increase his incarceration time or be resentenced.

He was currently on a nine-month program and had been locked up for almost six months. During this time, he had not earned one day off his sentence. On my fourth day of orientation, I was talking with the other staff members about different juveniles in the facility to get a little background information on some of these kids and how they interacted with different staff members. I wanted to know more about this kid, so on one of my days off, I passed by where he lived. It was a relatively new apartment building in a lower-middle-class neighborhood. He shared a two-bedroom apartment with his mother, two brothers, and a sister. His mother worked at a minimum-wage job and was making just enough to get by. I wondered why he would not want to go home to this setting and maybe help his mother by getting a part-time job.

On my next shift, I thought it was time for me to have a talk with this kid to find out why he did not want to go home. I approached him and asked questions as to why he was committing all the stupid little incidents so he would not earn credit to go home early. He said he liked it there.

This stopped me in my tracks. This sixteen-year-old kid liked being locked up and would rather be in jail than at home? My world was shattered. Here I thought I would be able to save these kids, put them on the right path, and help them become law-abiding citizens. Never did I think that someone so young would want to stay locked up. Boy, was I mistaken. I asked him why he wanted to be incarcerated, and his comment to me was, "Here I have my own clothes, my own bed, three meals a day, and all of my friends are here."

My vision of saving the world with these kids was totally altered.

It's a Family Affair

We all know the idiom "A family that prays together stays together." Well here's a new one: "A family that does drugs together goes in and out of jail together." You are probably wondering what I am talking about. I'm talking about "a family affair"—a mother, a son, and a daughter who had very little, if any, problem with being repeatedly incarcerated. Yes, the mother and both adult children alternated going back and forth to prison.

The story goes like this: The brother and sister were on parole and were required to come to my adult basic education class for a minimum of four hours per day five days a week. They were both unemployed drug users. Their parole agent wanted to know where they were for part of their day and had hoped that learning some basic skills would allow them to maybe get their graduate equivalency degree (GED) and possibly employment. They both showed up to class daily for the first three weeks, and then one Monday the sister did not show up to class. In fact, she did not come for a whole week. I had to report this to her agent after she missed three days. I asked the brother what had happened, and he informed me that she had gotten arrested over the weekend and would probably be sent back to prison. When I spoke with her agent, he confirmed that she had gotten arrested for being high on crack cocaine, and he had violated her (sent her back to prison). He said she would be gone for about six months but that her mother would be taking her place in class. The mother had just been released from prison, and the agent wanted to keep tabs on her because she, too, was an unemployed drug user. This was okay with me because this would maintain my student count—lose one, gain one.

Six months passed, and the sister was released, but now the brother was arrested and sent to prison for the same parole violation. He too was given six months. I found this to be curious: every six months one member of this family would violate parole and get sent back to prison. It finally dawned on me why they were doing this. I wanted to get more information to confirm my suspicions, but I decided to wait until I could speak with the son because my relationships with the mother and daughter were not as good as the one I had with the son.

When the brother returned six months later, I asked what the deal was with the three of them alternating their time going back and forth to prison on parole violations. With no shame, he told me, "Our family enjoys doing crack cocaine, so when we start to run out of money, we alternate going back to prison. If we get at least a six-month violation, upon our release we each get two hundred bucks in gate money. We put that money together with whatever money we have been able to hustle, and we buy and smoke crack."

I asked him why they did not mind going back to prison. He stated that, because they had been doing this for so long, six months was easy; no worries about having to hustle for food and shelter, and they felt safe because they had been doing this for a while. Additionally, when they got out, they had a blast smoking crack. This was more than a family affair; this was an institutionalized family.

I Need to Go Back to Prison

Some people spend so much time in prison that being free is too much work. With so many decisions to be made, some convicts get so confused and frustrated they cannot handle the reality of being free.

After spending eighteen years in prison, one ex-convict was paroled to the office where my class was located. His parole agent brought him to me, not for educational purposes, but for life skills help. His agent wanted me to help him acclimate back into society. I told the agent that I had some life skill curricula that I could work on with the parolee. During the intake process, the parolee and I had a good conversation about what we would be doing together. We completed the necessary forms, and we did some initial testing. We discussed his life and how he got started doing the things that got him sent to prison. We spent time talking about his childhood and how he had got caught up into the life of crime. Most of his family members were either incarcerated or dead as a result of living the street life. He shared that, as a little boy, he thought he was tough and wanted to impress his elders who had made names for themselves in the neighborhood. He was twenty-two years old when he was arrested for bank robbery and attempted murder of a police officer. I cannot imagine what a twenty-two-year-old experienced in a maximum-security prison, especially when his sentence continued for eighteen years. Plus, it had been his first time being incarcerated for anything, and he was doing hard time.

The first few days in my class were okay for him. He came in every day, we talked, and he completed his work. On Friday of that first week, I noticed that something was wrong. I asked him if there was something he wanted to discuss, and he said he didn't need to talk; he would try to work it out.

When he came in on Monday, I smelled alcohol on his breath, and I told him that drinking before class was against the rules. He would have to go home and come back the following day after he sobered up. I informed him that this was his first and only chance to not be reported to his parole agent for violation of classroom rules. However, because he was not categorized as a 5B (no use of alcohol), his second offense would get him removed from the program.

I can only assume that his first week of freedom did not go well for him. It must have been traumatic. When he came back the next day, he was somewhat distraught. He was crying like a small child. I asked him what was happening with him. He stated that he did not know what to do in the mornings. He did not know what clothes to wear. He was not sure what he was supposed to eat. What he was supposed to do on the weekends? He had problems working the remote for the TV, and he had no idea how to use his cell phone. He stated that being "out" was too hard for him because he did not know what he was supposed to do.

He thought he would get a job, but the only thing he had done in prison was clean, and someone had always told him where and what to clean. On top of that, he did not know how to even look for a job. I explained to him that I would help him with these things, but it would take a little time for him to get acclimated to being free. I had his parole agent come to my office and sit with us to attempt to help him work out a plan. That day, his agent took him to a car wash and got him a part-time job. This was something to keep him busy along with coming to visit with me every day before or after work.

On the Monday after his second weekend of freedom, he came to class drunk again saying, "I can't do this. It's too hard." I reminded him about coming to class drunk. I told him that, if he went to work that way, he would be fired. I informed him that he needed to go home before I called his agent. He said "fuck you" and stormed out of the class. I thought he was going back to his place, but instead he went next door to the parole office, pulled out a knife and yelled, "I'm going to kill everybody in this fucking place!"

Well, you can guess what happened next. Agents stormed into the lobby with guns drawn and arrested him. Before they could handcuff him, he swung the knife at an agent and struck him in his vest. Using a weapon in an attack on the agent along with shouting his terrorist threats were enough to get him sent back to where he would be comfortable. He no longer had the concern of having to handle freedom or make decisions. He got his wish. No more stress of being free. This is one example of a person being truly institutionalized.

Fat Butt Boy

Teachers of adult basic education in a parole office encounter something different every day. There is always something new to be learned from parolees, even things you do not want to learn or know.

On one Monday morning, I enrolled a sixty-four-year-old White male who had been told to report to me by his parole agent. I found out this parolee had spent more than fifty years of his life in and out of juvenile hall, jail, and prison. This parolee was very street smart, and he enjoyed reading and completing crossword puzzles. He had not finished high school and was not working. His parole agent thought it would be a good idea for him to attempt to get his GED just to keep him busy. His agent wanted him in a place where he would know where he was a few hours every day.

After testing this parolee, I believed that it would not take too long for him to pass the GED test if he put in some effort. He was far from being unlettered. I was thinking that it would take less than two months if he worked at least two hours a day getting his skills to the point where he could pass the GED test. His shortcoming was in math. During his first few weeks in class, we had many conversations about his life, prison life, his prison experiences, and the transgressions that had got him locked up. Most of his arrests were due to drugs. He told me that he was a large-quantity meth cook, which got him locked up repeatedly. He said he ran a major meth lab and that his business made thousands of dollars a day. I asked him how he had learned to cook meth, and he said he had learned from his father when he was twelve years old. I was curious to learn how he knew when the meth was done or cooked enough. He told me, "When you throw a six-pack of beer in the pot and the cans melt, it is done." I thought, *Wow, with all that aluminum in the mix, no wonder meth users don't have any teeth.* This parolee had no fear about going back to prison because he had spent most of his life there.

I noticed that every morning he was dropped off to class by a pretty young girl driving a relatively new car. She looked young enough to be his daughter. I asked him about her, and he said that she was one of his girlfriends. After his class time was up, another lady picked him up. She was middle aged, not bad looking, and drove a late-model Mercedes. I was thinking that maybe this was the younger woman's older sister or some other relative. I inquired about this lady, and again he stated that this was one of his ladies. I did not take the conversation about his love life any further.

As time passed and he was getting closer to taking the practice test for his GED, he started to miss his class time. Instead of coming every day three hours a day as was required of him, he would come maybe two or three times a week. I told him he needed to come every day if he wanted to stay out of jail. He said that prison was no big thing for him; that was where he had spent most of his life anyway. I made the comment, "What about the two nice-looking ladies you have? Won't you miss them? Are you willing to give up their companionship and go back to prison? You know there are no women in prison." His comment to me was, "There's no better joy than a fat butt boy." He said he liked boy booty better than sex with a woman, but he was not gay. He said, "I'm only gay in prison." Institutionalized? Well, I would think so.

I Miss My Cellmate

It was a normal day in my classroom. Some students were working on their math skills, others were working on their essay-writing skills, and others were testing. A parole agent interrupted the class by bringing me a new student for me to enroll. He was a nice looking thirty-two-year-old biracial gay man who was required to attend class until he found a job. This parolee had just been released from prison for drug possession and prostitution.

After testing this parolee, I found him to be of average intelligence but somewhat lacking in his math skills. Every day he would come to class, and we would talk about different things. He told me his mother was Black his father was White, and he had grown up in a middle-class home. His father was a school principal, and his mother was a teacher at the same school, which was where they had met. He talked about how he'd had a normal childhood until he was nine years old when he met an older man who was a friend of his father's. This man would come to his house often and give him candy and a quarter. One day he came over and, instead of giving him candy and a quarter, he gave him five dollars in exchange for the boy letting the man play with his penis. As a little kid, he liked the money, and he did not care if the man played with his penis. After a few times, he kind of enjoyed it.

When he was eleven, his parents divorced because his mom found out that her husband was on the downlow (having sex with men). She moved back east somewhere and did not keep in contact with her son, leaving his dad with custody. After a while, the man who was a friend of his father's played a game with him called "You kiss mine and I will kiss yours (penis)."

As time passed, while the boy was living with his dad, the man introduced him to another man who also played the game for money. After a few years, the man introduced him to men who would give him money for oral and anal sex. The parolee said that, until he was in his late teens, he did not see anything wrong with what he was doing, and the money was good. That was when he realized that he could make a lot more money doing the same things on the streets, so he then dropped out of school and started prostituting full time. He realized that he could make a good living doing what he knew how to do—having sex with men. He made a lot of money working the streets until he got arrested.

At first, he was sent to juvenile hall, which he thought was a joke. When he turned eighteen and went to jail, he met a man who told him he would take care of him when he got out.

When he was released from jail, he met up with this man, and they lived together for almost two years. They had a good life together until his lover became abusive. He told me the only way he could get out of this relationship was to fight back. He said one day his lover started beating him, and he fought back and almost killed him. He beat his lover so badly that he was in a coma for almost four months. The parolee got five years in prison for that.

During his last three years in prison, he fell in love with his cellmate. According to him, this was the man he had been looking for—the love of his life. Unfortunately, his lover was doing a twenty-year term. All this parolee talked about was how he could get back to his cellmate. He came to class one day and told me he had figured out what he needed to do to get back to prison to be with his cellmate. After listening to him explain to me what he planned to do to get back to his lover, I reminded him of the secret he had told me—he had AIDS—and they would not allow him back to the same prison. I told him he would probably be sent to another prison. There was no way of knowing where he would end up.

Unfortunately, he did not listen to me, and he beat up a female parolee in the parole office. He ended up back in prison, but I have no idea if he got back to his cellmate. However, he did get his wish of going back to prison. Institutionalized indeed!

I Can Do the Time if It's Not Long

This day was really no different than any other day in the classroom. The students who were required to attend class were there and had arrived on time. Some were complaining that they did not need to be there because they could read and do math. However, these students didn't have jobs, many of them were sex offenders and drug users, and their agents needed to keep track of them. New students were coming in all the time and had to be tested. Many of the parole agents came in regularly to check on their parolees and pick up a weekly attendance report. As I was preparing reports for the agents, I overheard a conversation between two of my newest female students. These were two White women in their mid-thirties. They were average looking, but I could tell that they were long-time drug users. Their hair was stringy, their skin was blemished, they had missing teeth, and they had tattoos on their necks, arms, legs, and other places. I could tell that they had been around the block a few times. These two women had been busted for drug possession and prostitution within two days of each other. They had never met prior to this class, but they had connected because they were the only two women in the class at the time.

As they were talking, they seemed to be comparing notes on the people they knew in the prisons where they had been incarcerated. They found that they had some of the same girlfriends (sexual girlfriends) and had had sex with some of the same correctional officers. They considered these officers weak. These correctional officers would allow them to have phone calls, and they would do other things for the female inmates if the inmates would give them blow jobs. They were laughing at the fact that, if they wanted extra stuff, all they had to do was have sex with the cops (their term for correctional officers).

I do not think that this part of their conversation was something they wanted me to hear, so I pretended not to be listening. When the subject changed, it was about how much time they thought they were going to get when they went to court. They were talking about how thankful they were that their parole agent released his hold on them and allowed them to get out of jail. They knew they were going back to prison and did not really care, but their concern was how much time they were going to get and where they were going to be held. One woman said, "I hope I only get ninety days because I can do that with no problem, but if I get more time than that, I will have to find me a bitch or some sucker cop to take care of my needs." The other woman said some of the same things but was hoping that, if she got more than ninety days, they would send her back home. She said, "If I have to do a lot of time, my bitches are waiting for me to come back home. When I left, they knew I would fuck up again and end up back home."

I assumed that "home" was a familiar facility where she had a girlfriend waiting for her along with some weak correctional officers who would be at her disposal. Women are no different than men when it comes to being institutionalized.

Prison Doesn't Scare Me

This particular morning was a good morning with my students. One of the students passed one of his lessons on the first try and was excited. It meant that he was really learning something, and he felt a sense of accomplishment for the first time in his life. Everyone in the class was giving him high fives because they were happy for him. I felt good knowing that I had helped another person accomplish something. My favorite agent walked into the class to bring me another student; he described this kid as an arrogant asshole who thought he knew more than anyone around him. He wanted me to keep him busy for at least four hours a day and maybe get him to pass his GED. He was a nice-looking Black man, twenty-eight years old. His very pretty Asian girlfriend sat patiently while we went through the process. He was nicely dressed, sported expensive jewelry, and drove a new BMW. However, he did not have a job. When his girlfriend asked to use the bathroom, my antenna went way up because her English suggested she had not been in this country very long. Was this guy a pimp? Where had he got the money for his car, clothes, and jewelry?

He completed the intake process and tested a little above average. He said he could pass the GED that day if I were to give him the test. The agent was correct. He was an arrogant asshole who thought he knew everything.

With my suspicions on high alert, I casually brought up the subject of how expensive his clothes looked, and that got him started. He bragged about his clothes and how much they cost. He said his jacket was by Diesel and cost him $800, his Nikes had cost $289, and his jeans had cost $200, and he had at least ten pairs. He said he would not tell me what his jewelry was worth because he didn't want me to be jealous. I was not sure if these things were original or knockoffs, but whatever they were, they looked expensive, especially for someone with no job. When I mentioned the fact that he had no job, he said he did not need one because his girlfriend was taking care of him.

I have always tried to be straight with my students and always attempted to show them the right way. I explained to him that, from what he was showing me and the way he was acting, there were at least two things I could tell about him. I said I could be wrong, but when I saw those things, I knew his agent and others around him saw the same things. I said he was either pimping, selling drugs, or both. He laughed and said, "You're no OG [original gangsta]! You're just a teacher and don't know nothing!" I told him I had grown up in the hood and I had forgotten more game [street sense] than he would ever have. I told him that I saw more things before I was twelve years old than he had probably seen in his twenty-eight years. I told him that, if I knew his game, his parole agent was probably aware and was waiting for him to slip up. He said, "Man, prison doesn't scare me. I've been there, and it was no big thing. I can do time standing on my head. Plus, my game is too tight, and I won't get caught." I was not sure what he was into, but I knew it was not good and it would not last long. His actions made me more curious as to what was in his file, so I wanted to read it and talk with his agent.

When I spoke with this parolee's agent, I asked to see his file. I read it and found what I had expected: he had been imprisoned for pimping, drug dealing, and domestic violence. He had spent three and a half years in a minimum-security prison, which I believe is why he said prison was no big thing. His agent was sure that he was back at it again but had no proof.

The day after my conversation with this parolee, he stopped coming to class. After he missed three days of class, I informed his agent that he was AWOL. The agent was not surprised but was unable to do anything for thirty days. Then, if the parolee did not report, he would be considered a parolee at large (PAL), and the search for him would begin.

A few weeks later, the agent came to my classroom and informed me that the kid had been arrested. He had been caught in a large drug operation by the Drug Enforcement Agency (DEA). The agent told me that the brother of the parolee's girlfriend was a big-time cocaine importer and that the parolee became a major player in the brother's organization in order to distribute drugs in the Black community and any other places he could.

When the agent spoke with the parolee, the parolee told the agent that he was glad to be going back to prison because he felt safer in prison than out on the streets. This was because of some of the things he had done to folks on the streets. To him, prison was easy. In my mind, this is an institutionalized mentality.

3

Death—Inside and Out

Choose Life!

—Deuteronomy 30:19

Death is something that we all know will eventually happen to us. We die from natural causes, old age, diseases, illnesses, accidents, car wrecks, drug overdoses, and many other circumstances. You hear about people being murdered over something like money, sex, or revenge; killed during a robbery; or killed by gang violence or drive-by shootings. Lately, we hear about people being killed by the police.

All of these events are part of life. We see this every day, and unless a death affects us personally, we see it as another revolution in the life cycle. We see it, hear about it, experience it in our families and with our friends, and ultimately, we continue with our lives.

It was not until I started working in correctional institutions that I saw a correlation between being incarcerated and death on the streets. Many of these deaths are due to greed, jealousy, revenge, or just plain meanness. I know from experience that people who are incarcerated sit around and plan the illegal things they will do when they return to society. I have personally seen these discussions and heard the plans. In many cases, death has been the result of many of these illegal schemes.

Pizza Robber

At one particular juvenile facility I worked at, there were two dormitories: one dorm, known as the kiddy dorm, housed boys under the age of sixteen, and the other dorm housed older boys. One day, I was assigned to the kiddie dorm. Many of these kids did not quite understand that they were in jail and that this was not a summer camp. They did not quite realize that this was just the beginning of what could happen if they continued their current life paths.

The youngest kid in this facility was an eleven-year-old Asian kid. His older brothers were gang members, and they were in prison; this kid thought that was cool and could not wait until he could go to prison too. He got his first stripe for committing a carjacking, and if he continued on that path, it would not be long before he would be joining his brothers.

This story, however, is about a young man who was in the kiddie dorm of the juvenile facility for the crime of strong-armed robbery. He was a fifteen-year-old Black kid—intelligent, a good student, and a good athlete. He was above-average size for his age, and he thought that, because of his size, he could take what he wanted from anyone he wanted— if he was his age or younger. I saw potential in this kid as a student and athlete, and I had many conversations with him. The responses he gave to my questions made me think that we had made a real connection. He told me he wanted to play baseball, go to college, and eventually get a degree in business. He also told me that his mother could not buy him all the things that many of his friends had, and he felt bad about that, so he decided to take things from those who had what he wanted. We discussed the consequences of doing things that way, and one of those consequences was the fact that he was locked up and could not go home.

I was really attempting to help him to realize that what he was doing was going to keep him locked up, and he would never play baseball or get to college. I spent many of my shifts mentoring him in the areas of setting goals, aspiring to be the best that he could be, and not taking shortcuts. We discussed at length that, if he wanted something, he had to work for it, not steal it or take it from someone smaller or weaker than he was. I really believed that I had gotten through to this kid. The day he was released, he said that he would try to do right, but if that did not work, he said, "If you don't get caught, it's okay." This was not something that I wanted to hear him say upon his release.

A few months after he had left the facility, I was told that he had been killed. The report was that he had devised a plan to rob pizza delivery guys. He had scouted different locations in his neighborhood that had either fences, bushes, or places where he could easily hide and then jump out to surprise the pizza delivery person. This was his method of operation: he would call for pizza delivery to a target addresses. When the delivery guy arrived, he would jump from his hiding spot, point a gun at the pizza guy, take his cash, and take off.

He had worked his plan in the same area at least four times when the police decided to set up a sting. He always called the same pizza company and had the pizza delivered around the same area. On his last robbery attempt, he followed the same MO. He called for the pizza to be delivered, and when the pizza guy showed up, he jumped out of the bushes with his gun, but this time, the police were waiting for him. When he brandished his gun, the police opened fire and killed him.

The irony of this story is that he was using a toy gun. In one of the last conversations this kid and I had, we discussed how using weapons when committing crimes would lead to more jail time or getting killed. He got killed.

He Should Have Stayed in College

In some juvenile facilities where I worked, there was an area called the honor dorm. This was a separate space with seven beds for exceptional juveniles who represented the population of the facility. In order to be in the honor dorm, the juveniles had to be nominated and voted in.

The counselors would review the files of the nominated juveniles, and those who were eligible would be voted on by their peers. Once a juvenile was voted into the honor dorm, he was responsible for keeping the peace amongst the other juveniles and for bringing grievances to the counseling staff.

To be removed from the honor dorm, the juvenile had to do something really stupid; otherwise, he would be there until he was released from the facility. Upon the juvenile's departure, he would be allowed to nominate his replacement.

One of the honor dorm juveniles was a special kid. We will call him Lawyer. He was a seventeen-year-old Black kid who had graduated from high school at the age of sixteen. His file showed that he had a GPA of 2.95, and all of his classes had been college prep. He was a really smart kid, but he got caught selling large quantities of cocaine in his neighborhood. When we had our talks, he confessed that he had become addicted to the fast life because of the money. He said he could buy anything he wanted and that the girls liked him because he could take them places. He said that he could have sex with a different girl every day if he wanted. This kid was "the man" in his hood.

This was his first time being locked up, and he said being in jail took those "perks" away from him, but that, while he was in jail, he would learn to be a different man. He said that, while he was there, he would work to help the other kids do better, which would help him to do better. He said that he wanted to do something with his life other than deal drugs.

Lawyer was on a mandatory sentence in this facility. He had a year to do, and he wanted to make the best of his time. He felt that he could make his time go by faster if he helped the kids with their write-ups (rule infractions).

Juveniles on a program could get their time reduced if they followed all the rules. For every day that they went without a rule infraction, they earned a day of freedom. Whenever a juvenile received a write-up (rule infraction) and he felt that the write-up was not justified or that it was excessive, he was allowed to write a grievance. In the grievance, the juvenile could explain why he felt he did not deserve the write-up and/or why he felt the write-up was wrong or excessive. Depending on how well it was written, the counselor determined if the write-up would stand or be dismissed. If the grievance showed that the write-up was not valid or incorrectly written, the write-up would be removed from the juvenile's file, and he would get his days back. All write-ups and grievances were reviewed by the supervisors, and the supervisors had the final say as to whether a write-up would be enforced or dismissed.

Lawyer was almost that—a lawyer—at the facility. Whenever a juvenile would ask Lawyer to write a grievance for him, Lawyer would, in most cases, get the grievance granted, and the write-up for the juvenile would be removed.

Most of the juveniles in the honor dorm were pretty good at helping the other juveniles write their grievances, but Lawyer was the best. In most cases, the staff members made mistakes by not getting the facts correct or not stating the proper infraction or not being able show cause for the write-up. Lawyer address those issues.

Lawyer was considered the honor dorm attorney. He won more grievances than he lost because his writing skills were, in many cases, better than those of some of the staff. Lawyer was so good that, when staff members saw he had written a grievance, they would, many times, remove the write-up or change it to a warning.

The Probation Department worked with an organization that had access to a college down South. This college provided second-chance opportunities for troubled youth and even gave scholarships to those who qualified. The requirements were not as stringent as those of a regular college, but the degree programs were accredited. The requirements were rather simple: high school graduate with a minimum GPA of 2.0, minimum SAT score of 800, and no violence on their record. Lawyer met all these requirements.

When Lawyer and I had conversations about him going to college, he did not think he could meet the requirements. I spoke with him about going to a local junior college, and he said that would be hard because the school was close to his neighborhood, and his reputation would be known there. That would not work for him. Also, there were too many distractions so close to home, and it would be too hard to explain to the boys in his hood that he had changed. However, he said that he did want to change and do something with his life other than sell drugs.

I talked to him about taking advantage of the opportunity at the college down South. He would be away from his boys and the neighborhood, and he could make new friends who had the same goals that he had. I stressed that, with his skills as a writer and communicator, he could be an outstanding lawyer or whatever he wanted to be, but in order for him to achieve any of this, he had to go to school and study hard. I informed him that two other young men in the program had qualified to go, so he would be with some people that he knew.

With staff support, he decided to give college a try. He said that he had talked with the other two guys who were going, and they had set up a plan for success. They felt that, if they kept to their plan and stuck together, they would all be okay.

With their acceptance to the college program and school starting in August, the guys were allowed to forgo the rest of their sentences to start school on time.

The staff gave them a going away party and wished them well. To ensure that the guys would not change their minds, instead of allowing them to return home, we had their parents and guardians bring their things to the facility. We helped them pack and took up a collection that provided each kid with $150. In addition, the Probation Department gave each of them $200. All the staff members who knew these kids were excited to see juveniles they had worked with go off to college. We all felt proud of their accomplishments as well as our own.

After the completion of their first semester, we got the progress reports on the guys we had sent away to college. One of the guys had come home after only a month. His mother had passed away, and he felt he had to return home to be with his younger siblings. The other juvenile was doing well, but Lawyer, although his grades were very good, was associating with people who were not on his level academically but had his street smarts. They were not really interested in school but were looking for a new place to renew their criminal activities. Lawyer, being as smart as he was, thought this would be the perfect place to do what he knew how to do and go to school at the same time. This lasted for a while until one night he and his new crew went out and were busted for possession of cocaine. With his arrest, he was immediately removed from the school and sent back home.

When he got home, he did not last long on the streets before he was sent back to the Boys Ranch. We were all disappointed but were not willing to give up on him. When we talked with him, he said that he had seen how easy it was to do what he had done at home and how much more money he could make there. He thought he could do both—get an education and make money, but he was not as smart as he thought he was, and he found he couldn't do both.

He was released after six months and went back on the streets. He hadn't been on the street more than six days before he was almost killed when he was robbed and shot seven times. Fortunately, he survived. Unfortunately, six months later, he was shot again, but this time the attacker made sure he was dead; he shot Lawyer in the head.

Many of us—counselors, mentors, and educators—had seen so much talent in him, but it all went for nothing. Thinking that you are smarter than those around you can be deadly. In Lawyer's case, it certainly was.

Pimping Is a Deadly Game

My assignment on this day was to transport juveniles from juvenile hall to the Boys Ranch. I had four juveniles to transport: two fourteen-year-old Asian kids, one fifteen-year-old White kid, and one seventeen-year-old Black kid. The three younger kids were going to the kiddie dorm (dorm for youth under the age of sixteen), and the other two juveniles were going to the regular dorm.

We will call this young man Toby. He was a well-mannered, polite, soft spoken seventeen-year-old, unlike the other kids from the ghetto. What really caught my attention was the fact that this kid had manicured nails. The only men I knew from the hood who had manicures were businessmen, drug dealers, or pimps, and for a seventeen-year-old to be this well-manicured, I just felt something was up. I thought Toby was either a drug dealer, a pimp, or maybe a gay prostitute. I would have to read his file when we got back to the facility to be sure.

When we arrived at the Boys Ranch and the kids were checked in, I immediately went to the office to read the file on this young man. What I read was exactly what I suspected; this kid was a pimp. He was pimping girls aged sixteen to twenty-three.

Of all the criminals that I have encountered over my lifetime—burglars, thieves, gang bangers, murderers, and anything else you can think of—I had never met a seventeen-year-old pimp. I wanted to get a better understanding of this young man. I wanted to know who he was. I wanted to understand the how, why, and who that had got him involved in that lifestyle.

I knew I just could not walk up to him and ask him his life's story, so I had to establish a relationship. After a few days, I watched the people with whom this kid associated. I knew and had relationships with most of his associates. On Sunday, which was visiting day, Toby and some of his friends were in the recreation room playing dominoes. I was observing them play when one of the kids got a call for a visit. When the kid left, I asked if I could join in the game since they had lost a player. Because I had relationships with the other two kids, they allowed me to join in. When I introduced myself, Toby said, "I remember you. You brought me here from juvenile hall." I complimented him on his good memory, and he then said, "My boys tell me that you are cool for an OG [original gang-sta]." I just told him I tried to be real with everyone there, and that I was there to help. From that point on, we had occasional casual conversations, and I learned where he lived, who he lived with, and what he liked to do.

A few weeks later, on a Saturday afternoon when most of the kids were outside playing basketball, he was in the recreation room sitting by himself reading a book. I walked over and asked him what was happening. He said not much, so I asked if I could sit and talk with him. He nodded and said sure. We started talking about things he liked to do, places he had been, and school. He said he liked school and rarely missed a day. He told me that he always got good grades because his mother did not want a dummy for a son. It surprised me to find a kid who was a pimp and wanted to go to school. I'd have thought he would rather be on the street dealing with his girls.

Little did I know.

When we started a conversation about his family, there was a change in his attitude, almost as if he was proud of something. He told me that, when he was three years old, his father was murdered during a robbery and that his dad had been a bigtime pimp in the neighborhood. He said that, when he got old enough, he wanted to be just like his father; however, his mother told him that the only way he would be able to do that was to go to school every day and get good grades. This was a bigger surprise to me. I had never heard of a mother telling her son that he could be a pimp if he did well in school.

Every day when I came to work, I wanted to spend time with this kid to find out more about his life. He was a good student even at the Boys Ranch school. I asked him, other than his mother not wanting a dummy for a son, what did he see as the benefit of going to school. His answer shocked the hell out of me. He said, "School serves two purposes. One is that I can get an education—especially math so I can count my money and not get cheated." I asked what the second benefit was, and he said, "That's where all the girls are." Not only was this kid book smart, but he had street smarts well above those of most adults with whom I had come into contact.

The answer to my next question was my biggest shock. I asked him where he had learned the pimping game, and he answered with no hesitation that his mother had taught him the game. He said his mother had been his father's "main bitch" and that his father had taught his mother the game so, if something happened to him, she would be able to continue the business and not have to work for another pimp. I had heard of older men teaching younger men the game, but never had I heard of a mother teaching her son. "After she taught me the game, she started to work for me. It's a family affair," he said.

He also told me that, now that he was locked up, his mother was handling the business until he got out, and that once he was out, she would have to go back to work. I had never heard stories like this—mother teaches son the pimp game, son pimps mother, mother takes over business while son is locked up, son gets out, and mom becomes a prostitute again. Never in my life, to this day, have I heard of anything as disgusting as this.

He told me that he had eight girls working the street, ages sixteen to twenty-three. They each brought in $300 to $500 a day. When he was arrested, he had in his possession almost $1,000. Ironically, he had not been arrested that time for pimping, but for domestic violence. He had beat up one of his girls, and she had called 911.

This kid was smart. He was able to talk the judge into sending him back to the Boys Ranch, which he knew was like a daycare facility. He received a ninety-day program and knew how to work it so he would be home in forty-five days. I really liked this kid, but I knew that there was not much that I could tell him that would get him to change his ways. He was a pimp like his father, and his mother was his main support. I never stopped trying to work with him, though, and always gave him food for thought.

Three months or so later, word came to the facility that Toby had been murdered during a robbery. All I could say was, "Like father like son." I wondered how the mother was handling this reality, losing both husband and son to the "pimp life." Pimping can be deadly.

They Won't Take Me Alive

It was the first of the month, and I was in the classroom putting together my monthly report numbers, which had to be submitted to my district office by the third of the month. I had come in early before my students arrived so I would not be disturbed. Just as I was getting started on my report, a parole agent saw me in the classroom and brought in a new student for me to enroll. This was *not* a typical student. When the agent introduced us, he spoke directly to the parolee and said, "You *will* attend this class every day from nine in the morning to two in the afternoon without leaving. If you leave for any reason, the teacher will contact me immediately." The parole agent said that he would be checking the parolee's hours every day, and if he missed any class time, he would be violated and sent back to prison. The agent then said, "Do you understand what I've just told you?" The parolee just looked at the agent with an angry look that was more intense than any I had ever seen before. The agent then repeated his question with a raised voice, "Do you fucking understand what I'm fucking telling you?" The parolee responded with, "Fuck, yeah."

When the agent left, I started the intake process. It took the enrollee almost two hours to complete the intake forms that most completed in only thirty minutes. He took the rest of his time that day to work on the testing process, and he did not complete the test. He mumbled the entire time he was completing the intake forms and taking the test. I could not understand what he was mumbling about, but I could tell he was angry.

I had been teaching parolees for a number of years and had never had a feeling like the one induced by this particular parolee. The way he had responded to his agent sent chills down my back. Based on this weird feeling I was experiencing, I knew I had to read his file to see what he was all about.

He was forty-five years old, White, six foot two inches tall, and weighed about two hundred pounds. He had large muscles and multiple tattoos all over his body. Some of his tattoos represented gang affiliation with the skinheads. His record indicated arrests for bank robbery, grand theft, and attempted murder just to name a few of the crimes this man had committed. He had spent twenty-one of his forty-five years behind bars.

In prison, he was a bad actor and spent a lot of time in solitary confinement. He had just been released from an eight-year term for armed bank robbery. The feeling I was having about this parolee was warranted—this guy was bad news. For the first time since I had been working with parolees, I was facing one who scared me, but I could not let my fear show.

The parolee followed his agent's directions for a good three weeks, after which he came to class one day very angry. I do not know why, but he was talking to himself saying things like, "They won't take me alive this time!" and "They will have to kill me before I give up!"

As a concerned teacher and one who had major reservations about this parolee, I asked him what was happening with him and if there was anything I could do to help. His response was, "Fuck my agent! He doesn't give a shit about me. All he wants to do is control my life, and I'm not having it. He can kiss my White ass. I'm going to do what I do, and they are not going to take me alive!" I had no idea what he meant, so I left a message for his agent to call me so I could report what this parolee had said. I was not sure if he meant to kill someone or if he was planning to commit suicide by cop. (Suicide by cop is a term used when someone provokes police officers to kill him by not surrendering while brandishing a weapon.)

Unfortunately, the agent did not get back to me for several weeks, and the parolee had not returned to class since that day. It turned out that the agent had been transferred to another unit and was no longer responsible for the parolee, and none of the other agents knew who this parolee was or what had happened to him.

Two months later, I was in the copy/mail/ dead file room, and I noticed the parolee's name on a file stacked on top of other files that were labeled "deceased" in big red letters. My curiosity got the best of me, and I had to find out how he had died.

After I read the reports in the file, his repeated statement "They're not going to take me alive" finally made sense to me. He had been planning another bank robbery and was willing to die instead of going back to prison. I had no idea what his agent had to do with all of this, but the parolee got exactly what he wished for—he was not taken alive.

Killer Athlete

The Boys Ranch ran multiple sports teams—volleyball, basketball, softball, and flag football. These teams would play teams from other juvenile facilities and some of the local high schools. To become a member of any of these teams, a juvenile had to be performing well in the program and not have any major write-ups. The counselor assigned to each player had to sign off and allow the juvenile to play on a team. In addition, each participant had to try out. Many kids wanted to be on the teams just to get off the Ranch, but they had no or very little athletic ability.

However, one particular kid who had tried out for the football team had extraordinary athletic abilities. He was a sixteen-year-old Black kid, five foot eight, about 180 pounds, and lightning fast. We clocked him in the hundred-yard dash at 11.1 seconds on grass. He was an all-around athlete and played on all our teams, but football was his favorite. His speed and his ability to catch almost any ball thrown his way gave him an advantage over almost any kid he came up against. However, the kid had one disadvantage—he was considered a special-education kid and was behind in school. He was sixteen years old and was going to be a freshman in high school.

He had missed two grades because he had mononucleosis when he was in the fourth and fifth grades, which caused him to lose those two school years. He was older, bigger, and stronger than the other kids in his classes, but he was always in trouble because he was teased about his size and the fact that he was not as smart as the other kids who were younger than him. This caused him to have anger issues, which resulted in him getting into fights all the time.

His fighting was what had brought him to the Boys Ranch. His file showed that a teacher gad provoked him by calling him stupid, and he had beat the teacher up pretty badly. Because he was a minor and had been provoked by the teacher, he had been sent to the Boys Ranch, and the teacher had been fired.

In addition to working at the Boys Ranch, I was also the head freshman football coach at a nearby high school. Watching this kid perform in all the sports, I knew I would love to have him play for me and attend the high school where I coached. I imagined I could be his mentor and keep an eye on him, and he would be a great asset to my football team. I also planned to help secure the tutoring he needed to get his grades to where they should be. Every day I was at the Ranch, I worked with this kid, helping with his schoolwork and trying to recruit him to come to my high school.

Unfortunately, when it came time for his release, his mother moved to a different district, and he was not allowed to play at my school. He ended up playing at a rival school, and needless to say, this kid ran all over my team. He was bigger, stronger, and faster than any kid on my freshman team and most of the kids on our junior varsity and varsity teams. By mid-season, the kid had been moved up to the varsity squad and became an instant success.

During his second season on the varsity team, he really had an outstanding season. He was so good that colleges were sending scouts to watch him play, and he was only a sophomore. If he continued to play well and got his grades to where they needed to be, the sky would be the limit for this kid.

Tragically, the summer of that year, I got wind that he was in juvenile hall awaiting trial for murder. When I heard this, I felt the need to visit this kid to find out what had happened. I knew he had anger issues, but not to the point that he could murder someone.

When I visited him, I asked him what happened, and I could feel the anger that was still in him. He explained to me that he had met this girl whom he really liked. He said he would take her places, buy her things, and do almost anything for her, but every time he attempted to have sex with her, she put him off. She said she was saving herself for when she got married.

While he was playing football, she was his girl. When football season was over, her attention went to boys who were playing other sports—basketball players during the winter and baseball players in the spring. Although they were still going together, she flirted with these other guys. He said this made him angry, but he liked her enough to let her do this because he thought he knew that she was still his girl.

During the summer, when he had more time, he looked forward to spending time with his girl, but instead, she broke up with him for no apparent reason other than she wanted to spend time with other people. This made him angry because, in his mind, she must be seeing someone else, and that was why she had told him to leave her alone.

He told me that, the next morning, when he went to her house to try and get back with her, he saw a car that he thought he recognized parked in front of her house. It was the car of a basketball player. He had gone to see her early in the morning because he knew that her parents worked, and when he saw the car, he started to get angry. The closer he got to her house, the angrier he became. He went around the back of the house to where her room was located, peeped through the curtains, and saw her having sex with this guy. He went to the front door and was going to break in, but the door was unlocked. He said he ran into the room, pushed the guy out of the way, and started beating and choking the girl. When he came to himself, she was dead. He said that, when the police arrived, he was holding her and crying, saying that he was sorry. The guy he had pushed out of the way had called 911.

After hearing his story, I knew that there was nothing that could be done to save him from a long prison sentence or the death penalty. He was now eighteen years old and would be tried as an adult.

So much talent and potential gone to waste because of his uncontrollable anger and issues over a girl.

Dead in the Shower

Would you ever think that there would come a time when no one in the world wanted you? Can you conceive of a time when everyone you know—family members, friends, and even your enemies—would disown you?

Well, for one parolee, that time had come. He was a forty-eight-year-old White male with tattoos all over his body representing the prisons where he had spent time.

He came from a middle-class family. His mother was a secretary; his father had been an electrician. He had a twin brother who was a real estate agent and a younger sister who was in college. Unfortunately, his father had died in a car wreck on his way to work when the parolee was ten. The father had been the backbone of the family and had taken care of his wife and kids. Soon after his father's death, life started to spiral downhill for this parolee. His father's guidance was gone, and he went out of control. At age twelve, he started drinking, at which time he met kids who were smoking marijuana Then, at age sixteen, he started using cocaine with this same crowd. And at eighteen, he started with meth. His last stop at age twenty was heroin.

His first arrest was at age twelve for being drunk in public. From that point on, he was in and out of juvenile hall, jail, and finally prison. Once he started using heroin, his drug habit got so bad that everything he did was for the sole purpose of feeding his habit.

Early on in his drug usage, when he was not in prison, he stayed with his mother and stole from her to buy drugs. When she finally kicked him out, he went to stay with his twin brother and even stole from him. His brother wanted nothing to do with him after a while, and he kicked him out. His last stop was his little sister. It got so bad with her that she had to get a restraining order to keep him away. He took her savings, stole her credit cards, and put her in debt. She had him arrested for breaking into her apartment and stealing her money and jewelry.

It got to the point that all his family members and friends had restraining orders on him, so he was not allowed to be around anyone he knew. Even the neighbors had him banned from the neighborhood because he had broken into their homes in order to feed his habit.

His excessive drug use had taken a toll on his body. He was as skinny as a rail, most of his teeth were gone, his hair had fallen out, and he had track marks on almost every part of his body. He looked worse than your typical junkie. I have no idea why he was sent to the program at the prison, but he was. I think his parole agent hoped that, if he got locked away for ninety days, at least he would not have to think about him.

He arrived at the in-prison drug program in mid-December, and on New Year's Day, he was found dead standing in the shower. When the call was placed to his next of kin, his mother said, "You guys have had him most of his life, so you handle him in his death. I don't want anything to do with that motherfucker."

This came as a shock to all those who were involved with this guy— the parole agents; correctional officers; and teachers, including me. We had never encountered a situation in which no one wanted to claim a family member's body.

I guess when you misuse and abuse all your loved ones for an extended period of time, they will eventually turn away from you in life and even in death. At least that was the case with this man.

Death Without a License

I have been a teacher for many years. I have taught kids how to play soccer, football, and baseball. I have taught my own five kids how to read, write, count, do math, tie their shoes, and many other things that most of us teach our kids. My plan was to become a high school teacher, but I ended up teaching for the Department of Corrections teaching adults basic skills, reading, writing, math, and GED preparation.

One Monday morning, a parole agent brought me two students who were mother and daughter. Both were lacking in basic skills. The mother was a sixty-year-old Black woman, and her daughter was forty-four years old. The mother's reading level was at third grade, and the daughter's was slightly higher at fourth grade.

The problem I saw with this situation was that the mother had been only sixteen years old when she had her daughter. She had probably already been behind in school and dropped out at whatever grade she was in at the time. I can only assume that, when it was time for the daughter to go to school, the mother had no clue what she was supposed to do and was unable to help with any studies as the daughter advanced in school.

Both mother and daughter had been in and out of prison because of drug use and prostitution. Neither of these women worked, so their agent required them to be in class daily for three to four hours.

They were good about coming to class and were working hard to improve their skills, especially the mother, but occasionally the mother did not show. When I asked the daughter where her mother was, she said her mother did not have a car. This went on for some time. Every time the mother did not show up for class, she had lost her car. When she came back to class, she would always have a different car.

After the fourth time this happened, I asked the mother to tell me her story about her and her cars. She explained to me that she did not have a driver's license, and whenever she was stopped by the police, she got a ticket for driving without a license and some other infraction and her car was impounded. She stated that it cost less money for her to buy another cheap car instead of getting her car out of impound. We then discussed her taking the test to get her license, and she said that she had taken it at least twenty times over the past five years and had not been able to pass the test.

When I asked her why she was always getting stopped, she stated she would be speeding or running a red light or doing something else reckless that would result in her getting a ticket; and because she did not have a driver's license, the police would impound her car. She said that she always paid her tickets and that she needed to drive to get to the places where she had to go. She said she knew how to drive but just did not know all the rules.

For the next two months, the mother and I worked on the Department of Motor Vehicles manual to get her to pass the driver's test. Because her reading level was so low, and her retention was almost nonexistent, I suspected it was going to take quite some time to get her to the point of passing the test. We even worked on attempting to memorize the answers to some of the old tests, but that was not working either. She would get some of the answers correct, but then she would get confused.

I was determined to help her get her license. I gave her some material to study over the weekend and told her to bring them back to me on Monday. These were simple words that would be on the test, but I had arranged them in a way that I hoped she would be able to understand.

Monday came and neither the mother nor the daughter showed up for class. I assumed that the mother had gotten another ticket and her car had been impounded so she had no way to get to class, but the daughter was not there either, which was unusual. I went to talk with the daughter's agent to find out where she was and found out that she was back in jail for prostitution and drug possession. She would soon be going back to prison.

Several weeks later, I was reading the newspaper when I saw an article reporting that my student—the mother—had been killed in a car wreck along with the driver of the other car. The story reported that she did not have a license and that she had been stopped on numerous occasions for driving without one. The journalist suggested that someone should have known that this woman was a menace and that she should have been locked up and the key thrown away for driving without a license.

The only reason this woman did not have a license was that she could not read and could not pass the written test. What would be the difference if she had a license? The accident still would have happened, and two people still would have died. A license would not have saved their lives.

Sad but true.

I Want to Be with My Folks

In the juvenile system where I worked, all young offenders were required to attend school unless they had already completed high school. Most of the kids were behind academically, and attending school helped them to catch up with some of the credits they needed to graduate. The school helped them at least to attempt to keep up with their graduation requirements. However, there were some kids who were so far behind, they would probably never catch up or meet the graduation requirements. Those who were eighteen years old were not required to attend school.

This story is about one of those kids who, sadly, would never in a lifetime catch up.

It was a normal Saturday at the Boys Ranch, and not a lot was happening. The boys had just come back from breakfast and were having their quiet hour, writing letters, reading, or just relaxing on their beds waiting for free play to start.

One of the juveniles asked permission to come to the counselor's booth. I gave him permission. The kid needed a new pair of shoes because the soles of the ones he was wearing had come apart. Every piece of clothing was accounted for, so when a replacement was needed, a form had to be completed. I provided him with the form and asked him to fill it out. I told him I would then get him a new pair of shoes.

This was an eighteen-year-old Black kid. He had turned eighteen while serving his time at the Boys Ranch, and he had been in the facility for over a year. When he was three years old, his mother had died of a drug overdose, so he had spent most of his life going in and out of foster care. Most of his male family members had been in and out of prison. His father, grandfather, and uncle were all currently on death row. This kid had dropped out of school in sixth grade and started committing petty crimes, most of which were drug related or robbery. I often saw him around the facility but did not have much interaction with him. He seemed to avoid me whenever I was around, and I believe he did this because he did not want me to know he was not smart.

When I talked with some of the kids from his neighborhood, they told me that he was not smart but that he was a tough guy and could fight. Some of the other counselors informed me that he was very slow but wanted to be the toughest kid in the facility. Many of the kids made fun of him because he was mentally slow; these taunts caused him to get into trouble for attempting to fight. He never fought but would bluff as if he were going to fight.

When I handed him the form to complete for the replacement of his shoes, he gave me a puzzled look. I asked him what the problem was, and he told me that he did not know how to read. He asked me to show him where the word *shoes* was on the form. Now I understood what everyone was talking about. I showed him where *shoes* was on the form and told him to put an X in the box next to shoes and sign the form. Unfortunately, not only could he not read, but he could not even write his own name. I was shocked but not surprised that this eighteen-year-old young Black male was unable to read or write. How had he survived for so long without these skills? I completed the form for him and told him that I would get him a new pair of shoes. I went into the storage room, picked out his shoes, and wondered how this kid was going to survive once he was released from this facility. He was now eighteen and was no longer considered a child.

When I handed him his shoes, I asked him a few questions. The first questions were, "What are you going to do when you get released? You are now eighteen years old and are considered an adult. You can no longer be in a foster home, so where will you live? What kind of job will you be able to get so you can eat?" He told me, "I'm going to be with my folks." I was puzzled by this statement and asked him to explain. His mother had been deceased for fifteen years, his father was on death row along with his grandfather and uncle. I asked him what folks he was talking about. He said his father, grandfather and uncle. Knowing where they were, I was curious as to how he planned to get there. So, I asked him. He said with very little emotion, "That's easy. All I have to do is kill somebody while I'm robbing them, and I can be sent there with them." My heart slowed down from the shock at his comment, and I immediately stated that, if he saw me on the street, he must make sure that I was not the one he tried to rob and kill to punch his ticket to death row. He told me with sincerity that he would not kill me in order to get to be with his folks. "You are cool with me, so I couldn't do that to you."

Unfortunately for this young man, about three weeks after his release, he was murdered during an attempt to rob and murder someone else. It was unfortunate that he was murdered, but it might have been the best thing for someone who was illiterate with no basic skills and who had the desire to kill someone—anyone—just so he could be with his folks on death row.

Just Really Dumb Stuff

Deliver Us from the Fruits of Evil.

—"Evil," performed by Earth, Wind & Fire,
written by Maurice White with Philip Bailey.

The stories in chapters one through three were serious, but many things that happen on the inside are stupid and downright dumb. In this chapter, I will share some of these stories—situations that I feel were funny, dumb, and stupid. But you be the judge.

Athletic Shoes

There was this little sixteen-year-old Black kid at the Boys Ranch who was from a middle-class family but wanted to be a gangster. He walked around the Boys Ranch trying to act tough but would always get beat up. We never *saw* him get beat up, but we always saw the aftereffects—busted lip, black eye, and other bruises. Unfortunately for this kid, he was not very good at fighting; he was just a wannabe.

It was Sunday afternoon, visiting day. All week long, this kid had bragged that his father was coming to visit on Sunday and that he was bringing him a pair of Air Jordans. Indeed this wannabe gangster's father did come to visit that Sunday as promised, and he did bring the Air Jordans the kid had been bragging about.

Dumb question: Why would a father want to reward his son for being in jail with a two-hundred-dollar pair of athletic shoes? Well, whatever the reason, I felt it was irresponsible and dumb.

On Wednesday morning when the juveniles got up for breakfast, the wannabe gangster's new shoes were gone. After breakfast, the juveniles were instructed to sit on their beds. They were called up to the counselors' booth one at a time and questioned about the missing shoes. It was a school day, so we could not keep the kids long. We questioned as many as we could before school, and we continued the questioning after lunch and finished just before dinner. After we finished with our interrogations, we knew that the questioning had been futile because none of these kids would snitch on whoever took the shoes.

While the questioning was taking place, the rest of the staff members were searching the facility for this kid's shoes. We knew all the hiding places on the facility, but the shoes were nowhere to be found. We believed that, because this was an open facility, whoever stole the shoes had thrown them over the fence onto the road adjacent to the facility and had had someone come pick them up.

One would think that this would be the end of the story, but it was not. The wannabe called his father and told him that someone had stolen his shoes and that he needed another pair. The father brought another pair on the next visiting Sunday—dumb, dumb, *dumb*!

Thug Life

For many juveniles, it is a badge of honor to go to jail. In a lot of cases, juveniles are following in the footsteps of their incarcerated family members and friends. When a gang is involved, the kid gets his "stripes"—or clout—in the gang by going to jail.

This story is short but true. The juvenile, a Hispanic male, was fifteen-years old when he committed strong armed robbery of a twenty-year-old man. By the time he was sentenced, he had turned sixteen and was sent to the dorm for older boys at the Boys Ranch. He and his entire family were affiliated with the Surenos Street gang and wore the color red all the time. On her first visit to the Boys Ranch, the mother of this kid came to the facility flaming—wearing all red: shoes, blouse, pants, lipstick, and nail polish. She wanted everyone to know which gang she represented. Wearing gang colors in any facility is prohibited; therefore, she was not allowed to visit on that day or any other day when she wore her colors. To get around the not-wearing-red rule, she would always wear deep red lipstick and fingernail polish, which we could not control or censure.

I did not have any personal contact with this mom until it was time for her son to be released. I had seen her on numerous occasions during her Sunday visits, but we had never spoken. I was working the release desk on the day she came into the facility to pick up her son. She came flaming again, knowing there was nothing we could do because she was just there to pick up her son. When she approached the desk, she asked for her son, signed the release papers, and said, "I hope you guys fixed him after you have had him for a year so he won't come back to this place." This really pissed me off, and I said, "How the hell do you expect us to fix your son in a year? It took you sixteen years to fuck him up with all of the gang shit you have him involved in." I knew that, if she told my supervisor what I had said, I probably would have been fired, but I was totally pissed off. When her son came out and they were walking away, I noticed a tattoo on the back of her neck that read "Thug Life."

How dumb can she be? She wanted us to fix her son in one year while she had been living the thug life in front of him for at least fifteen years. Dumb, dumb, *dumb*.

GUESS

You are probably wondering *GUESS what?* Well, some people do stupid and dumb stuff without realizing that what they are doing is actually dumb.

It was Saturday morning at the Boy's Ranch, and most of the staff that day were female counselors, each of whom had less than two years of experience. One female staff member thought that she knew more than the older staff members, including myself. This was because she had passed the probation officer test and was awaiting her promotion. When she worked, she would do dumb little things like wink and blow kisses at the boys. On this particular day, she was wearing a GUESS T-shirt. As the kids were going to breakfast, one boy stopped, looked at the counselor's T-shirt, and said "I guess 32A". This pissed off the counselor, and she gave the juvenile a major write-up in an attempt to get his time extended.

The juvenile wrote a grievance and won. Not only did he maintain his original time, the counselor was transferred to the girls' facility at juvenile hall, all because of dumb stuff like wearing a GUESS T-shirt at a juvenile facility filled with young boys. After that incident, no one was allowed to wear any shirt with logos. Everybody had to wear Probation Department shirts.

Guess Again

Educated people are not always the smartest people. One would think that, if a person had been chastised once for being dumb and stupid, he or she would not do anything to jeopardize his or her position within the system ever again. Well, some people just do not get it.

Our GUESS counselor was now a probation officer; she worked on the streets and not in a facility. She was responsible for checking in on her kids at school or at home any time day or night and any place day or night. With this much freedom, what do you think Dumb or Dumber would do? Well, she became the dumbest person I ever knew.

I was working the three in afternoon to eleven at night shift at the Boys Ranch when I got a call from a mother of one of the juveniles who had spent time there at the Boys Ranch. The juvenile was now on probation, and the mother was calling the facility asking where her son was. She stated she thought that her son was on probation and should be home every day after school. She said that some lady who said she was his probation officer would pick him up from school and sometimes would not bring him home until late at night. She wanted to speak with the person in charge of this "probation lady." It was 10:30 at night, and no one at the Boys Ranch knew anything about who this kid's probation officer was or where this mother's son could be. We told the mother that someone would have to get back to her the next day because there was no one from the Probation Department at the Boys Ranch at that hour.

Because I was the one who took the call, I was responsible for writing the notes for the administrator. When the administrator read my notes, he called me and wanted any additional information I could give him. I told him that I included everything I knew in my notes. He then asked me if I knew a certain probation officer, and I informed him that I did. He wanted any additional information I had on her. I told him about the GUESS incident and suggested that he should probably speak with person who was her supervisor when she had been a counselor there at the Boys Ranch.

It was four months later when the news came back to us that this probation officer had been busted for having sex with more than one of her wards. The dumbest part about this was that she always used the same motel and the same room at the motel. She had rented the room six months at a time. When officers crashed into her room, they caught her in the act of having sex with one of the youths entrusted to her care. When the wards were questioned, they all told the investigators that they did not mind having sex with their probation officer, and that she had told them she would send them back to juvenile hall if they did not comply or if they told anyone.

Again, how dumb can one be? An adult having sex with teenagers does not think that they will tell anyone? Dumb, dumb, *dumb*.

New Tattoo

This story took place in a minimum-security, ninety-day drug rehabilitation facility. Unfortunately, the inmates did not have a choice about being there. Either they went to the program or they would be parole violated and could spend a year or more in a level-two or -three prison.

Many of the hard parolees in this low-level prison thought that the rules were different from the rules in more secure institutions. They thought the guards were soft and no one would pay attention to minor rule infractions. Unfortunately for these parolees, many of them did not last and were violated. Once it was known within the inmate population that this prison was not a joke but the real deal, the parolees followed the rules to the best of their abilities. However, there were always a few who thought they could get away with what they considered to be little things.

It was the beginning of the week, and I was doing my usual Monday morning walk through the dorms, making sure that the guys were up and moving around to get ready for class. One of the parolees whispered to me that there was a tattoo gun in one of the dorms.

As in all prisons, inmates group together by race: Whites, Mexicans, Blacks, Asians, and Pacific Islanders. I asked the parolee what group had the gun, and he said the Skinheads, who were part of the White group.

I had a quick meeting with my teachers before class started and put them on alert to be on the lookout for any White parolee with a new tattoo. A few minutes after class started, I got a call from one of my teachers.

When you talk about dumb stuff, this would be at the top of the list. The parolee with the tattoo was the "shot caller" for the White Nazi group. He had shaved his head and had two lightning bolts tattooed on his scalp. Nothing could be more obvious than this—White guy with swollen tattoos on the top of his head. When I sat down with this parolee, I explained to him that he had violated the program and prison rules by having contraband in the facility. While we were talking, I was having his locker searched for the tattoo gun. The report came back that it was not in his locker. With this information, I proceeded to tell the parolee that, without the tattoo gun, he would be removed from the program and, due to his parole violation that had him sent here in the first place, he would spend at least a year at another prison. I explained to him that I needed to have the tattoo gun. He said it was not his and he did not know who had it.

I gave him an ultimatum: bring me the tattoo gun by lunchtime or pack his stuff to be removed from the program. Additionally, I told him that, if he did not bring me the gun, everyone would be strip searched and anyone else with a tattoo would also be removed, and he would be responsible for his removal. In other words, he would be considered a snitch. Being considered a snitch in prison could result in death or a good beating: snitches get stitches. I told him that, because he was the first one to be caught with a new tattoo, he was responsible for having the tattoo gun in the facility and would be charged with the contraband. I sent the parolee back to class. I then had to inform the lieutenant what had transpired with the parolee and the decision that I had made. He agreed with my decision, and we waited to see what would happen at lunchtime.

Lunchtime arrived, and so did the parolee with the tattoo gun. He was asked by the lieutenant why he would tattoo his head knowing that everyone would notice. He said, "I didn't think anyone here would care if I had a new tattoo." The lieutenant responded, "Did you forget that you are in a prison and it's against the rules?"

Just dumb stuff.

Eraser

One would think that a person working in a prison surrounded by two hundred plus inmates would not do anything stupid that would get him or her hurt. Some people just do not think—or they forget where they are and who they are surrounded by.

It was a Wednesday afternoon, and one of my teachers was having a bad day in the classroom. The video reorder was not working right, so she could not show the intended video. I provided an alternative lesson for her to give to her students until I could replace the video machine. The students became a little restless while working on the alternative lesson, so I helped the teacher with the class for a while.

As the day progressed, I noticed that this teacher was having issues with some of her students. She had worked in prisons before, and I thought that she would know how to deal with unruly students or students who were not following directions. I called her to my office during the next break to talk with her. She stated that she was having issues at home with her fifteen-year-old daughter and was somewhat distracted. I asked her if she needed some time off to handle her personal business. If she did, she could use her sick leave. She said she would take the next two days off and come back on Monday. She said that she thought this would be enough time for her to settle things with her daughter.

On Monday morning, I spoke with the teacher before classes started and inquired about the issues with her daughter; she informed me that her daughter wanted to go back home and live with her father. She said that her daughter did not like living in a new town and was having a hard time with the kids at school.

I monitored the teacher throughout the morning to see how things were going. We spoke again at lunchtime, and she seemed to be okay. As classes resumed, I was going to each dorm posting the new independent study schedule for the parolees. As I returned to my office and was about to take my seat, the teacher rushed in and said, "I think I messed up." I asked her what she meant, and she said, "I tried to get the students to take their seats and they ignored me, so to get their attention, I threw an eraser at them and hit one of the students in the head." I thought to myself, *How dumb can you be, lady? You are in a prison surrounded by thirty inmates and you decide to throw an eraser at them?* I told her she needed to go back to class and apologize to the student she had hit and to the entire class. I then asked what lesson she was teaching, and her response was anger management. I advised her to use this as a good teaching moment, and to explain to the students that what she did is *not* the way to handle any anger situation. I advised her to give them examples that would illustrate the best way to handle what had happened. I told her that she would also have to acknowledge how inappropriate it was for her to do what she did.

As she left my office, I became really pissed off. There was no way she could clean up this mess by apologizing to these students during an anger management lesson. They were convicts in a prison school, and the teacher had just exhibited the same lack of self-control that had got them there. Before I could figure out what I should do next, the lieutenant called me into his office. He informed me that the teacher had to go; in other words, she was being walked off the facility and would no longer be allowed on prison grounds.

I asked the lieutenant if the warden would be satisfied if I was able to get her to resign immediately. I brought the teacher back to my office and explained the situation. I told her that she needed to resign immediately, and that if she did, she would be able to keep her credential. If she didn't, a report would be made, and it would be attached to her credential, and she would not be allowed to teach anywhere in California.

Throwing an eraser—or anything else—at an inmate in a prison is dumb, dumb, *dumb*. She could have been beaten—or worse.

Escape # 1

It was a normal day in the prison program. There had been no incidents, all teachers had issued good reviews of the day, and the morning teachers had gone home. The evening shift of teachers, who provided independent study for the parolees, was to start at 5:30, and independent study classes were to begin at 6:00. Most of these teachers had day jobs, so on occasion they were a little tardy. I did not have a problem with them being tardy once in a while as long as it did not become a habit.

I have made the statement a number of times that most inmates are not smart. This situation involved an inmate who was downright stupid, but also scared of repercussions. Why would anyone escape from prison to return in the same night?

Well, let me tell you what happened. This facility was a minimum-security prison surrounded by a twenty-foot cinder-block wall. There were what looked like peep holes in different sections of the cinder block wall, and the top of the wall was armed with razor wire. On the other side of the wall there was a ten-foot fence topped with barbed wire. This fence surrounded the wall, and between them was a walkway everyone called, no man's land. Between the fence and the parking lot was a thirty-foot span of grass.

Because the parking lot was so close to the wall, a family member or friend—anyone with an average arm—could easily throw contraband over the wall; in fact, throwing contraband over this wall was almost a weekly occurrence. Correctional officers routinely walked around the facility in no man's land to check for drugs and other paraphernalia that had not made it over the main wall.

One evening, I was standing in the yard talking with a correctional officer when a racket ball came flying over the wall and hit me in the back. The ball was filled with baggies of marijuana. I have that ball to this day, marked with the street name of the individual for whom it was intended.

Whoever threw the package over the wall got it only over the fence, and the package landed in no man's land. This had to be a planned event that did not go very well. We knew this because, when the person expecting the package did not get it, he and his boys started looking through the peep holes in the wall. Eventually, they saw the package flat on the ground in no man's land. The person waiting for the package was a forty-nine-year-old White male who had a long arrest record. He was a shot caller—a person in charge of a set, race, gang, etc. He ordered a young White inmate, who was only twenty-three years old and had done only one prison term of two years for multiple car thefts, to scale the wall and retrieve the package. It was never determined exactly how he was able to scale the wall, although there was some speculation of how it was done. Also, we wondered how he been able to climb over the razor wire and then climb back in without major wounds.

The inmate retrieved the package and was climbing back over the wall when one of the evening teachers, who was arriving late, was entering the building. As he approached the entrance into the prison, he noticed the inmate climbing back over the razor wire. The teacher did not believe what he was seeing; he could not believe that someone was climbing back *into* the prison. When he entered to start his shift, he informed me what he thought he had seen and was confused as to what he had just witnessed. I immediately informed the sergeant on duty. The sergeant and I both knew what this was about, but we could not fathom that someone would actually attempt something so stupid. We had to find the inmate and the contraband that had been tossed over the fence before it was spread throughout the facility. Our next action was to get everyone out in the prison yard and ask who the culprit was who had climbed over the wall. We knew that no one would admit to escaping and returning, and no one would snitch on the escapee.

The sergeant then had everyone strip naked. I was not sure why he was doing this until he explained to me that there was no way a person could climb over razor wire without getting cut up. That made sense. After everyone stripped, we found our escapee. He had multiple razor cuts on his legs, arms, buttocks, and back. Our next task was to find the contraband that the escapee had retrieved. He had not had time to get rid of the contraband, and it was not too difficult to find—it was in his locker. The bag contained drugs and cell phones with chargers.

When we asked him why he had climbed the wall, he stated that he had been forced to do it, but he would not tell us who forced him. We knew who the shot caller was for the White inmates, but with no proof, we could not charge him with anything. We also knew that the escapee had been forced to keep the contraband in his locker so the shot caller could not be implicated. He also stated that, had he not followed the orders of the shot caller, he would have been severely beaten, so he felt he could not refuse. The shot caller also told him that he would not get caught because no one would be around; he said all the evening teachers would be in class, and they would keep the officers preoccupied. This was a true statement except for the fact that one teacher was late to work. Had the teacher been on time, they would have gotten away with it. The really sad part of this story is that this kid had only two weeks left in the program and would have gone home. He was not yet a hardened criminal, but he had been forced to follow orders. Now he was facing charges of escape and possession of cell phones and drugs in a prison. If convicted, he would be doing a long stretch in another prison, all because of a stupid stunt. I asked him if the beating he would have received would have been better than the time he would have to serve. He said, "Yes. I should have said no, but in prison that is not an option."

Escape # 2

A number of prisons have fire camps on their grounds. These facilities house inmates who help to fight fires and assist with other projects in and around the surrounding community.

The prison in this story was a minimum-security facility. There were no cells or bars, and the dorm doors did not lock. These inmates were well fed; they had much better food than was served behind the wall. The inmates were able to enjoy the fresh air, and they ate, slept, and worked together. This was as close to freedom as an inmate could get while serving time. Not just anyone could apply to be in the fire program; they all had to earn the right to be participants by having perfect records while they were in the general population.

On this spring day in April, not much was happening at the camp. My teachers and I were running a training session in the conference room at the fire camp when we received word that an inmate had walked away from the camp. Because this was an open facility, it was very easy for anyone to walk away. However, because of the stringent selection process to get into this program, walking away had never been an issue of much concern.

On this particular day, a thirty-six-year-old White inmate who had been in prison for four years and had done so well that he was allowed to become part of the fire camp, decided he was ready to leave this place and go home. It did not take long for the inmate to be apprehended because he was walking around the city in his prison uniform.

When he was brought back to the camp, he was asked to describe the events of the day and why he had tried to escape. He started the conversation by saying that he had missed Mother's Day for the past four years, and this year, he wanted to be home with his mother. He said he had walked down the hill, and when he had reached the bottom, he realized that he could not get far going in that direction. He walked back up the hill to the road that intersected with a bike trail. By walking down the bike trail, he thought he could get into town. On the road, he met a biker and asked him for a cigarette. The biker said he did not smoke, and the escapee continued on down the bike trail. Unfortunately for the inmate, the biker was an off-duty deputy sheriff. The sheriff called the prison and told them that an inmate was walking down the bike trail trying to get into town. The inmate was apprehended by California Department of Corrections and Rehabilitation personnel and was brought back to the facility. When the inmate was asked what he had planned to do once he got into town, he stated he was going to steal a car and drive home to spend Mother's Day with his mother.

This plan was not very well thought out because his mother lived in Oregon, and he had no money for food, gas, clothing, or anything else. The irony here is that he was being released in early June just a little over three weeks after Mother's Day. He would have been out and could have spent the rest of his life with his mother if he wanted to. Now he was being charged with escape and would have to go back to a real prison and would no longer have the freedom he had at the fire camp.

He was going to miss a few more Mother's Days.

Escape # 3

It was less than nine months later that another inmate attempted to escape from the fire camp. This inmate had put a lot more thought into his plan. He was a highly educated forty-two-year-old White male who had been in prison for six years. He was from Southern California and did not know much about Northern California. He had been part of the fire camp for two of those six years, and he knew all the ins and outs of the camp. We can only speculate that this inmate had some help because he had a stash of civilian clothes, some cash, and a city map hidden outside the boundaries of the prison. After he walked off the campgrounds and changed his clothes, he looked like an ordinary civilian walking down the street; because of this, no one paid much attention to him, and it was easy for him to hitch a ride into town. The inmate made it to a populated part of town, walked into a grocery store, and bought a pack of cigarettes. When he exited the store, he stole a bike that was parked in front of the store. He took off on the bike but had a hard time following his map. He rode around for a while, but he ended up not far from where he had started. He was stopped by the police because they were following him. When they asked him for identification, he had none. When they asked whose bike he was riding, he stated that it was his, but he could not prove it. The police finally informed him that it was a "bait bike" and that he had stolen it. He was arrested for bike theft.

When he arrived at the jail, he refused to talk. The police put him in a holding cell until they could identify him. While the escapee was sitting in the cell, the police received a BOLO (be on the lookout) for him and discovered that he was an escaped convict from the fire camp. Off to prison he would go.

His plan would have worked better had he known the area and/or had someone waiting for him with a car to get him away from the area. Stealing the "bait bike," which was secretly equipped with a global positioning system (GPS) device is what got him busted. His plan was only partially good. He was so close yet so far away from freedom. Well, at least he got to smoke a couple of cigarettes.

Wait Until You Get Home

When inmates who have spent at least six months in prison are released, they are given what is called gate money. They can use this money to buy bus tickets to get home. If they have a ride, they can use the money for whatever they want. Release from a ninety-day, in-prison program is a little different; there is no gate money given to newly released inmates. If an inmate does not have a ride, he is transported to his parole office or to the halfway house he is to enter. If he does have a ride, he is transported to the parking lot of the main prison to be picked up by a family member or friend.

In this story, the inmate was transported to the parking lot to be picked up by his girlfriend. He was a twenty-seven-year-old Hispanic male who had anger issues, especially when it came to women. He had been arrested on numerous occasions for domestic violence and drug possession. We did not know what the issue was with his girlfriend, but had this inmate just gotten into his girlfriend's car and driven off prison grounds, he would have been free and clear—well maybe. But *no*. He started an argument with his girlfriend in the parking lot before he got in the car. The argument got so loud that correctional officers who were parking their cars before reporting to work stopped to observe this argument to ensure it did not get violent. Well, it did, and he started beating on his girlfriend right there in the prison parking lot. How stupid can one be?

The correctional officers who were observing the argument went to break up this assault. As they approached the aggressor, he turned and started fighting the officers. It took four officers to control this newly released inmate. He was handcuffed and taken to a holding cell in the prison.

Now this newly released inmate was on his way back to prison. He got zero hours of freedom. This time it was not only for assaulting his girlfriend, but for assaulting multiple peace officers as well.

As he was being put in the van to go back to prison, he was informed that had he waited until he got home, he might have gotten away with assaulting his girlfriend, but instead he was going to do some hard time for assaulting the correctional officers. He was asked what they were fighting about, and he stated that he had been told that, while he was in the ninety-day prison program, his girlfriend had been sleeping around. He was asked who had given him this information, and he said that his sister and his ex-wife had told him the night before he got out.

Whoa, I think this was a setup. Somebody did not want him to come home, so she set him up. Not to say it would have been okay, but why not wait until you get home to figure it out?

Success

My Spirit is Undaunted.

—Barack Obama

The hope of many counselors, teachers, and other professionals working in correctional institutions is that those who are incarcerated will become valuable contributors when they are released back into their communities. When this happens, there is a sense of pride that flows through our bodies. We can look at that individual and say, "I played a part in the success of that person." It does not often happen, but when it does, we know that our work with these individuals has helped them and has meaning.

Many of these individuals wrote about what they learned in the programs they attended and what lessons they could use that would help them become successful. I've included two of these writings by inmates who made goals to be successful. Not all the end results in these cases are known, but what is known is that these parolees did not return to the prison program.

A New Life—A Poem for My Success

I spent my life thinking I was wild and free; all I was really doing was hiding from me.

I said forget my freedom and sanity, never mind my children, friends, and wife.

I'll live my way. It's my life; to hell with pride and dignity. I'll live in chaos and calamity.

Time passed, and my life grew more insane, finally the Program came.

Nowhere left to hide, nobody else to blame, a moment of clarity handed to me on a platter.

The Program teachers telling me it's not too late, and that my life really does matter. I can have a new life truly wild and free, filled with love, laughter, peace, and serenity.

I will look in the mirror with pride and dignity, and it all starts with my sobriety.

I do not know what happened to this individual, but if he continued the life he described in his poem, maybe he became a successful person in our society.

My Life—A Wake-Up Call

As a little kid, I was pretty much raised around drugs and violence. I started drinking beer and smoking pot with my parents when I was about eight or nine years old. When I was about fourteen or fifteen years old, I noticed my parents were getting into the heavy drug scene, slamming heroin, doing cocaine, meth, and other drugs. Around the age of sixteen, I started following in their footsteps.

By this time, my mother had become a prostitute so she could support the drug habits she and my father had developed. My father expected her to continue to do this and forced her to continue doing this. I began to resent my father to no end because of what he allowed/forced my mother to do. I had a very hard time accepting this because I knew it was morally wrong. Being a kid, watching all of this crap, and even being a part of it really screwed up my head.

As a scared little kid, I found my escape from the pain and reality that I no longer wanted to deal with. I started stealing, robbing, and hurting other people. I started selling drugs and committing heinous crimes. I would do whatever it took to get money so my mother would not have to go stand on a street corner, and I could support my own drug habit. Before I turned nineteen, I caught my first prison term. I did not give that number back until I was thirty-five years old [not being caught committing any crimes and off parole]. Not long after giving my number back, I was back in prison with a new number. Seventeen years of my life was given to prisons because of my drug use.

In the process, I've lost two of the most precious people in the world to me because of their drug use, my mother and father. No matter how much anger and resentment I held toward them, I always loved them unconditionally. I still do, and I always will. I have no choice but to do so; they were my parents. The moral of this story, which is a true story, is that drugs have done nothing but caused chaos and destruction in my life. They have caused death to my family and nothing but pain and hurt in my heart.

Well, I'm tired of hurting. I'm tired of hurting myself. And I'm also tired of hurting others. I'm also tired of everyone in my life suffering the consequences of my stupidity and selfishness. I've finally come to the realization that it's time to grow up and start taking responsibility for my own actions. I've got a lot of crap stuffed inside: anger, hatred, confusion, frustration, loneliness, hurt, and so forth and so on. It goes on and on, and I know in my heart that, at some point in time, and very soon for that matter, I'm going to have to start dealing with a lot of these emotions and feelings that I've been ducking and dodging for the past twenty years or more, especially if I'm going to choose to live a clean and sober life.

I've never been one to open up, share my feelings, or ask for help. I always seem to let my false pride get in the way of all that. Well, it's time to swallow that false pride. It's time to start humbling myself. And it's time to start asking for help. I truly want and need to succeed in living a clean and sober life.

About a month before my mother passed away, a very beautiful woman stepped into my life. She loved me for who I truly am, and she married me. That made me take a long hard look at myself. It made me look at the person I'd become as a result of using drugs, and it made me take a look at the real me, the person my wife fell in love with. Well, it's time to lose the person the drugs fell in love with, and it's time to be the man my wife fell in love with.

Believe it or not, I've slowed down a lot. I've come to realize that it's going to take more than just slowing down. It *all* has to stop. I've decided that here and now is when it stops.

As I said, I have a very beautiful wife, whom I love and respect, and three little boys whom I very much adore. I know that, without a doubt, they want me to be a part of their lives, and I very much want to be a part of their lives. It's time that I get out and make that happen.

I saw this parolee about six months after his release, and he said he was doing well. He said he had a job, and it was going well. He said that, in another three months, he would get a promotion and a raise if he continued to do what he was doing. Just maybe this parolee reached his goal of being successful.

From Juvenile Hall to the NFL

A new arrival to the Boys Ranch came in with a special condition: he was allowed to attend his regular high school to complete his studies so that he could graduate with his class.

I was curious as to what made this kid special. As I was reading his file, I saw that he was a college prep student with a 3.1 GPA. Also, he was an excellent athlete and had a scholarship to a Division I school. However, he had lost the scholarship because of his involvement in a home burglary, which led to him being sentenced to a year in juvenile hall. He was sent to Boys Ranch because this was his first offense, and he was not considered a hardened juvenile criminal. His file showed that he was a follower and not a leader. He just wanted to be one of the boys from his hood. However, when he was arrested, he was high on marijuana and had a weapon (a large knife), and that was what got him the year.

A number of high school football coaches worked at the Boys Ranch, myself included. We all knew that this kid had talent, and if we could keep him focused and in shape, there might be a possibility he could get his scholarship back or get one from another school.

We worked with this kid every day when he returned from school. We put together a schedule so the coach who was on duty knew what to work on. The plan consisted of speed work, route running, agility, weightlifting, and pass catching skills just to name a few. He seemed to want the extra coaching, and he said he appreciated the fact that we cared enough to do this for him.

A few of the coaches reached out to the contacts they had with colleges and were able to generate interest from a couple of their connections. Many of these scouts already knew about this kid and thought he was already attending a Division I school, but when they heard about what had happened, a few stepped back from wanting to look at him.

However, there were a few people who were still willing to take a look and possibly give him a second chance. When the scouts came to the Boys Ranch to watch him work out, they were impressed and said they would get back to us.

This kid was offered a scholarship to a Division I school three months before he was to be released from the Boys Ranch, which made all of us who were involved very happy. We felt that he could be successful if he accepted this second chance, and he was.

He kept in touch with us throughout his college career. When he came home on summer breaks, he would stop by the Boys Ranch and spend time with us, and he would always tell us how much he appreciated what we had done for him. He also talked to the kids about his life and how it had changed because he had listened to the counselors.

Because he was having such a great college career, he was getting a lot of attention from National Football League (NFL) scouts. When he finished school, he had a number of workouts with these scouts as well as with NFL teams. Unfortunately, he was not drafted, but one team took a chance on him and signed him as a free agent. He played a total of five years with two NFL teams. He played long enough to earn retirement income from the NFL.

I believe this is what one would call success: from juvenile hall to the NFL.

A Totally New Man After Eight Terms in Prison

You never know what motivates a man who has spent most of his adult life in prison to want to become a better person, but for this inmate, whatever it was, it happened.

This man had spent most of his adult life behind bars. He was tattooed from his wrist to his neck, and his head was bald. Anyone looking at him would automatically assume that he was a tattooed skinhead, but that was far from the truth. He was a very intelligent man who had a drug habit that kept him in trouble.

Due to his drug use, he was sent to my ninety-day drug education program. This man was just another parolee going through the program like hundreds of others had done. It was not until after his graduation that I had any real personal contact with him. He approached me one day and asked if he could return and speak to the group about what he learned from the program. This took me by surprise because no one from the program had ever wanted to come back and speak to the participants. The speakers we normally had were parole agents, wardens, correction administrators, school administrators, and people from community organizations—never a former program participant.

When we talked, he shared that he never had any idea why he was doing the things he was doing until it was explained to him in a certain way. He said that, over the past fifteen years, he had been required to attend many drug programs, inside and outside of prison, but ours was the first one that made sense to him—he got it.

He said that, in the program, he learned why drugs had controlled his thinking and why he was always so angry. He learned that there was a way to control his anger. He said that his one-on-one teacher helped him realize that he could make a change and become successful. He said that, after he listened to many of the guys in the program, he realized that they did not really "get it," and he felt he could help them understand.

This made a lot of sense to me. What better way to reach these parolees than to have one of their own talk to them? If it came from one of their own, maybe they would accept what we were trying to convey to them.

I made a deal with Fred. I told him that, if he stayed clean and sober for the next six months, I would consider having him come back to speak to the graduating class.

It was exactly six months to the day when the parolee called me. He said that he was clean and sober and had a job using the skills he had learned in prison. He said that he was working for a heating, ventilation, and air conditioning (HVAC) company, and that his boss was okay with the idea of him giving back to those who had helped him. He also said that he had enrolled in college and would be starting classes the upcoming semester. I told him that I would have to let him know. I needed to get approval from the facility lieutenant and the warden, and if they gave permission, the next graduation would be in three weeks.

It did not take much to convince the lieutenant and warden; we were all on the same page. They felt, as I did, that there was no better way to get a message across to these parolees than to have it come from one of their own, someone who had gone through the same program and who was currently working toward becoming successful.

On graduation day, the parolee did an outstanding job. He shared his story starting from the time he was a juvenile through his eight terms in prison including many of the crimes he had committed.

His story ended with what he had taken away from this program and how it was up to all the participants to take the information that had been presented to them and use it to their advantage, just as he had. He got a standing ovation, and many of the parolees wanted to talk with him afterwards. Fred spent an hour talking to these guys. This was impressive.

Fred agreed to come back and speak at three more graduations.

Each time, he added more positive information to his story—classes he had completed, promotions and raises he had received—and he always attributed his successes to the teachings and information he received from the Program.

On one visit, he informed everyone that he had be dating a young lady for a while and that now they were planning their wedding and were going to Hawaii for their honeymoon. He said that he never dreamed that he would be sober enough, out of prison long enough, or off parole long enough to think about going on a trip to Hawaii, and here he was getting married and going to Hawaii for his honeymoon. Again, he attributed this to his wake-up call he received while he was in the program.

It was almost nine months before I heard from this parolee again. During that time, I was concerned that something had happened that was not good, but I was wrong. He explained that he had been really busy at work, with school, and with his new life as a married man. He said he would like to come speak at the next graduation if that was possible. I welcomed the idea because I considered him as a true success.

On this visit, he did his usual thing of telling his story, showing his tattoos, and sharing how the program saved his life and made him a new man. However, that was not all. He ended by saying that his wife had given him a son two weeks before and that, after the graduation ceremony, he was going to sign papers for the home he was purchasing for his family.

His last comments were, "If you guys don't listen to what they have to offer here, you will stay in your rut and continue to be failures. I listened, and look where I am today."

I have seen Fred on the street twice since the program shut down, and he is still doing well. This parolee was a true success story and someone that I will never forget. He is a great example of the certainty that success is truly possible for anyone who really wants it.

Epilogue

After working in the correctional system for a few years, I came to realize that trying to save the souls of everyone incarcerated was not realistic. Based on the ages, environments, educational levels, and the criminogenic thinking of the inmates, and their desire to continue in these lifestyles, I realized that there was only so much that I could do.

With a renewed understanding of the criminal mind and the impact that the lack of education, dysfunctional environments, and the influence that family members and friends had on the inmates, I came to realize that I could help and rehabilitate only those people who wanted help and rehabilitation. Therefore, I concentrated all my efforts on those inmates who demonstrated that they wanted to make a change.

If I could change one life, I considered my work to be a success. Every day my goal was to try and save *one*. I was fortunate and can say that I saved more than one over a period of many years.

9 781665 734332